A DIFFERENT
KIND OF CHURCH

Peter Watherston

A DIFFERENT KIND OF CHURCH

The Mayflower Family Centre

...

Marshall Pickering

An Imprint of HarperCollins*Publishers*

Marshall Pickering is an Imprint of
HarperCollins*Religious*
Part of HarperCollins*Publishers*
77–85 Fulham Palace Road
Hammersmith, London W6 8JB

First published in Great Britain
in 1994 by Marshall Pickering
1 3 5 7 9 10 8 6 4 2

A catalogue record for this book
is available from the British Library

ISBN 0 551 02899-8

Typeset by Harper Phototypesetters Limited
Northampton, England
Printed and bound in Great Britain by
HarperCollinsManufacturing Glasgow

Contents

Foreword

IT HAS LONG BEEN my belief that we live in a very exciting period in the life of the Church. New ideas are emerging in many places as questions are asked about the role of the Church, its relationship with the community, appropriate patterns for mission and evangelism, the nature of liturgy, leadership, morality and culture, lay involvement — and so the list runs on.

Many of these are, of course, not new questions, though they may be being asked in new ways. Most, if not all, of them have faced the Church every time it has sought to be a channel of God's love to his world. But, sadly, in our generation's desire to grasp hold of the new, we sometimes forget the lessons of even the comparatively recent past.

My hope is that this book will be an antidote to some of those tendencies. Here is a rich quarry for anyone who wants to address such questions in the life of the Church today and to learn from the experience of their fellow believers. These pages tell the story of real people facing the real difficulties, and experiencing the real joys, of living out their Christian lives in their own community. That strand of honesty, coupled with a good dose of humour, runs through the chapters.

This is a book to wrestle with, to weep over, to rejoice in, to wonder at and to be challenged by as, in and beyond the human stories, it opens up a wider canvas of God's love and faithfulness. The Mayflower Centre is, of course, well known to me personally. As an East Londoner I know that its rich and distinctive ministry has been, and is, greatly appreciated. It is a story worth telling.

It is also a story with important lessons for the Church today. David Sheppard's words express my own beliefs when he writes: 'I want to encourage the Church to grow in two directions: to be outward looking, ragged-at-the-edges, involved in the messy and hurting human experience which our neighbours face, with plenty of stepping stones on which we may meet them. And at the same time to be a Church in which there is deep commitment to Jesus Christ, with our spiritual roots being refreshed both personally and in the fellowship of the body of Christ and as we serve him in a hurt world.'

God grant that we may increasingly become such a Church.

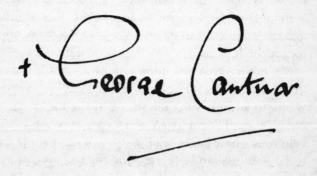

Introduction

WHAT JUSTIFICATION is there for writing this book? A number have already been written, both about the Docklands Settlement experience and the early Mayflower one, and these are listed in the bibliography at the end. Perhaps as a milestone such as a centenary is passed it is a reflection on the experience of a church working its way through a series of conflicting pressures, hopes and fears. Some of the lessons learnt may be of help or interest to others. The message is not for others to imitate what has happened here but to hear what the Spirit is saying to their own church and to trust Him to fulfil it — to be prepared to take risks, including the risk of failure in following the call of God.

'He who has an ear, let him hear what the Spirit says to the churches' is a phrase repeated in each of the seven letters to the Churches of Asia Minor recorded in the book of Revelation. In the current plethora of discussions and opinions about inner cities and urban ministry it is not easy to hear what the Spirit is saying. It is easier to opt for a life, activities and initiatives based on pragmatic assessment of needs, funding and convenience.

There have been three or four different 'Mayflowers' since it was formed in 1958 and a number of different 'Malvern Missions and Docklands Settlements' in the previous sixty years as the needs and circumstance of

Canning Town through peace and war, poverty and welfare state, employment and unemployment have changed. There have been times when the light has flickered very low and other times when it has burnt brightly. What binds the work together has been the constant desire to bring the reality of a loving God to bear on people's lives. This has been by word and worship and in social care and concern in practical outreach to the community surrounding the Centre. Has it been faithful in hearing what the Spirit is saying at each stage of its development? The reader will have to judge that for him or herself.

When this book was first suggested I was the only member of the Mayflower Council not to vote for it! We thought originally it would simply comprise contributions from people who had been associated with this place. We wanted in particular a strong voice from the East Enders who were and are involved in the work. The publisher felt it needed a narrative taking the story through, and the local church did not want a professional writer to do it. So with considerable reluctance I took the task on.

As well as the individual stories, the main text tries to reflect the contributions made by past and present staff, residents and local church members. Inevitably it will be weighted towards the views of those who responded to the request for contributions!

There is a sadness that some people felt unable to contribute, which might have provided a more 'rounded' account. In the end it cannot be objective. The way the story is presented inevitably reflects my own interpretation and prejudices. I hope this will not cause more hurt to any who feel misunderstood or ignored. The story cannot reflect every part of the work or mention everyone involved, and the absence of a reference does not imply that Mayflower is not deeply indebted to many, many people who gave of themselves here.

After the two initial chapters there are two for each of the three twelve-year periods of Mayflower's life — the first is more analytical, reflecting the events and the changing vision, the second recording more of the detail of the work and its effect on people.

Thanks are due to Sue Barley for recording and transcribing numerous interviews with local church members; to Edward Furness for cutting down the original material by nearly half; to Doreen Turner for getting the photographs together;and to Janet Gosling and my sister-in-law, Liz Matthews, for putting in so many hours typing the draft manuscripts. Thanks to Mark Birchall and John Oliver for their comments on the final manuscript. Special thanks are also due to all those who put time and thought into making the contributions.

Canning Town — a history

NO ONE IS SURE where Canning Town got its name. Some think it is linked with Lord Canning while others think it comes from the process of canning goods carried out in factories nearby. What is known is that a hundred and fifty years ago the area was fields and marshland bordered by the river Lea to the west running into the Thames at the south part of Essex. One main road which we now call the Barking Road crossed it running from East India Docks across Plaistow Marshes to the hamlet of East Ham and Barking with an iron bridge over the river Lea at Bow Creek.

London ended officially at the river Lea, but as trade exploded in the mid–1800s new docks and factories were built by the rivers. The Metropolitan Buildings Act did not allow certain offensive or noxious trades to be carried on within London's boundaries and many of them took refuge just across the Lea — oil boilers, gut-spinners, varnish makers and printers' ink makers. In 1855 the new Victoria Dock, the first of what are known as the Royal Docks, was finished and shipbuilding yards were established close by.

There was a big demand for labour and so Canning Town, Hallsville and Silver Town were created. This was done in a hurry with speculators buying up land and putting up cottages without drains, roads, gas or pavements. There is a graphic account of a visit to Canning

Town in 1857. The writer describes coming to a row of houses built with their backs to a stagnant ditch. 'We turn aside to see the ditch and find that it was a cesspool, so charged with corruption, that not a trace of vegetable matter grows upon its surface — bubbling and seething with the constant rise of the foul products of decomposition that the pool pours up into the air. The filth of each house passes through a short pipe straight into this ditch and stays there.'[1]

The effect of breathing such air day and night was that fever was constant. When an epidemic came it tended to stay for months and a local clergyman counted the burials in a period of six months in Plaistow and Hallsville which had equal populations. There were sixteen deaths in Plaistow and in Hallsville seventy-two. This state of affairs lasted much longer than it would have due to the corruption and delay of the local water company.

An Ordnance Survey Map of 1895 shows the area as teeming with tiny cottages. Often more than one family would share a home. Of course, there were no bathrooms and people preferred to sit outside all night in the summer rather than sleep with the bugs inside. One of these condemned cottages was kept on the Dockland Settlement site until the new buildings were put up, as a reminder of the terrible conditions people lived in. It was a small single room which had been occupied by a family of six. Edward Knoblock in his introduction to Kennedy Cox's *Autobiography* says: 'I know this room myself and the horror of it is still vividly before me. A greater indictment of the results of industrialization could not be imagined. In this room, eight foot square, half-a-dozen human beings had eaten, slept, lived and died under conditions that would lead to prosecution if applied to any domestic animals.'[2]

The story of the London Docks is a sad one. It was born out of the Industrial Revolution and was doomed from the beginning by lack of planning, an inability to control its phenomenal growth and a failure to coordinate the work as a whole.

The two major problems were that intense competition between dock companies forced port dues down during lean periods and that the variable number of ships docking and needing unloading and loading meant the dock companies could only afford a small number of permanent staff with the rest taken on twice a day at the 'dockers call' on a casual basis. This system lasted for one hundred and fifty years until 1967, and caused intense bitterness in labour relations.

In the beginning there were no unions and the calls were a free-for-all with men jumping on the backs of others to attract attention. There was shouting, fighting and struggling among thousands of men for only one day's hire. 'For weeks many went there, went through the same process, the same cries and went away after all without the work they had screamed for.'[3] The possibility of work and the cheap rents of the hovels of Canning Town attracted unemployed agricultural workers, victims of the Irish potato famine and countless Jews from Eastern Europe. Competition between the docks and the surplus labour had led the companies to force down wages to four pence an hour. This rate was held for over forty years. Trade unions came into existence to fight for more and they developed their numbers and muscle in a series of strikes. The dock owners usually tried to starve the dockers back to work and the hardship endured by many families during those strikes was intense.

Work in the docks was divided between the stevedores, known as 'the blues', due to the colour of their union card, who initially worked solely on board ship ensuring that the cargo was stowed securely and the dockers, known as 'the whites', who were responsible for transferring cargo to and from the ship's side. The stevedores belonged to the Nation

Amalgamated Stevedores' and Dockers' Union (NASDU) and nomination to the union could only be made through the applicant's father or paternal grandfather, or, if they had died, through another relative. Dockers generally belonged to the giant Transport and General Workers' Union. NASDU's practices which were often described as restrictive and elitist arose out of the bitter experience of depression and deprivation with no welfare state to cushion the hardship.

But the effect of the increasing militancy on the union side, combined with the continuation of casual labour even after the establishment of the National Dock Labour Board in 1948, was followed by the irony that a year after the docker had achieved his ambition of permanency and a basic minimum wage in 1967, the London Docks received its death certificate when the American *Lancer* came into Berth 40 at Tilbury and a crew of fourteen dockers discharged and loaded three and a half thousand tons of containers, equivalent to six days' work on general cargo requiring a hundred men. The ship was turned round before the next tide. Thus the advance of technology had done what the industrial strife and the Blitz could not do.

Canning Town and the area around was devastated by the war. The holocaust swept down upon the London Docks on Saturday, 7th September 1940. Soon blazing factories and smashing, crumbling houses brought home the terrifying danger of the situation to the bewildered workers and distracted housewives. The unquenched flames lit up the scene and pierced the safeguard of the blackout so that wave after wave of enemy planes could carry on the work of destruction. These intensive raids continued over two months of increasing strain. The most destructive bomb was the one that hit Hallsville School which was crowded with people waiting to be evacuated. A massive programme of evacuation out of London was arranged for all those

Old Rathbone Street Market - 1958

children of the borough whose parents wished it. Many families left, never to return. At the close of the Second World War over fourteen thousand homes had been destroyed in West Ham and many more damaged. Much of the maze of mean streets had been swept away.

So wholesale was the destruction that it enabled a fresh start to be made. South of the Newham Way in Canning Town and Custom House there is scarcely a house dating from before the war. However, new premises were built so slowly that by 1959 only just over a third of those destroyed had been replaced. This contributed to a change in housing policy. In 1961 the first three tower blocks were erected in Canning Town. At first glance this form of housing seemed ideal for the city, being inexpensive and using little land. However, complaints soon followed about faulty lifts, vandalism and the stress of 'high-rise' life. Many tenants formed action groups to voice their opinions and the explosion and partial collapse of one of the tower blocks, Ronan Point, in 1968 highlighted some of the dangers. No new blocks were built and by 1993 all but one of the eight twenty-three-storey buildings have been pulled down.

John Bourne came to Canning Town in 1970. He has written a vivid account of the more recent years.

My earliest memories are of traffic jams. To stand in Rathbone Market on a hot summer's day was to risk suffocation from exhaust fumes. Commuters to and from the city and heavy dock traffic all converged on that one spot. Pollution levels were high. By 1973 the Canning Town flyover and Newham Way were built. They were essential to relieve the Barking Road but this new main road had been driven through the middle of a community and the two halves linked by subways.

During the 1950s and '60s there had been much slum clearance and tower-block building but the construction of that road was probably the prologue to changes that few at the time could ever have conceived.

I worked in the London docks from 1970 to 1972. In 1970, within the Royal group of three docks, there were about 70 ships berthed at any time. In the Victoria Dock were meat boats from Australia and New Zealand, sometimes berthed three abreast. In the Royal Albert dock were passenger ships from South America and cargo ships loading for India and the Far East. The King George dock handled cargoes to and from many parts of the world. At the end of each dock was a dry dock. Near the main entrance to the Royal group was Harland and Wolfe's repair yard. Outside the enclosed docks were countless river berths. Ships brought raw sugar to Tate and Lyle's Silvertown refinery and others took cables away from AEI at North Woolwich. It was the men who worked the river and the tug boats who were amongst the greatest characters of the area.

Many Mayflower people worked in these docks. As I visited ships I would meet Rich Gerard loading a Ben Line ship with general cargo for the Far East or Keith Latch discharging the frozen meat carcasses from a Port Line ship recently arrived from New Zealand. To me those docks were full of fascination and an interesting place to work. To many Canning Town people they were the institution upon which their lives were dependent. Jobs were handed down from father to son. The whole heart and soul of Canning Town was in those docks. By no means everybody was employed in them, but most local residents were affected by them.

In the three years between 1970 and 1973 the number of ships in the Royal group dropped from around 70 to about 15. By 1980 a whole way of life was gone and countless lives were affected. Many, but by no means all of the best young people moved away.

If I visit docklands today I think of those ships. It's as though their ghosts haunt you. The vast flat space of the City Airport seems lifeless and inanimate as though a silent memorial to what had gone before.

■ ■ ■

The physical history of an area has spiritual consequences. In one of the great Old Testament prophecies, the Lord tells Ezekiel to speak to the mountains of Israel and to the deserted cities which were plundered and mocked by all the surrounding nations. He speaks of Israel's enemies gloating and saying: 'Now those ancient hills are ours!' (Ezekiel 36:2). Israel had been overrun and the people taken into exile and there was both a physical hold over the land of Israel and a spiritual one. Reconquering the land was not just a physical problem of building up armaments and men. It was a spiritual one involving a sovereign act of God which would include sprinkling the people clean from all their sins, taking away their stubborn hearts of stone and replacing them with obedient hearts of flesh and putting God's spirit in them so that they would follow God's ways. Then the people would rebuild the ruined cities and replant the wasted fields and the land which was once a wilderness would become like the Garden of Eden. Canning Town from its very beginnings has been plundered and mocked. It was built and developed to satisfy the increasing opportunity and desire for gain of the traders and manufacturers of London. Goods were sucked in from all over the world at the expense of the peoples of the countries they came from as well as of those who unloaded and worked on them here.

The people of Canning Town could echo Ezekiel when he says: '. . . it is true that people call the land a man-eater and they say that it robs the nation of its children'. (36:13). People here did not have any control over their own lives or those of their families. Discussions about jobs, pay, housing, health were always taken by people who lived elsewhere. Oppression is a way of describing limited choice and even the charitable action taken to alleviate hardship and poverty was decided upon and controlled from outside the area.

The human spirit, made in the image of God, is very strong. The courage and determination of many people to live under harsh conditions was great. The solidarity, the humour, the family loyalty were all there in abundance. The determination to oppose the dock owners even at the cost of increased hardship, the ever-open door to family, neighbours and friends if anyone was in need are legendary. Many people have commented on the East End community spirit. People did not have much but they shared what they did have with others.

In the end, however, when exploitation and oppression continue over a long period the spirit of the people is broken. That is the time when the enemy spiritual forces take such a hold that they can gloat and say: 'Now those ancient hills are ours!' The effect of oppression is apathy and rebellion. On the one hand a resignation, a dependency, running from any responsibility. It is as if the will has completely withered and is incapable of being exercised except to avoid the most obvious pain and take the easiest way out. On the other hand there is a rejection of authority, an increasing breakdown of acceptable behaviour expressed in crime, drugs and drink. Of course, there will always be exceptions. There are people who do take responsibility, bring up families, maintain standards, but they will be a shrinking number.

On top of those longer-term pressures came the devastation of the war. In the early '90s in praying for the area and the buildings God seems to have identified the spiritual effects these events have had even forty years later.

One of the continuing themes as you read the accounts of the foundation of the Malvern Mission right through to the present day is the hardness of Canning Town in its resistance to the gospel. Soon after the arrival of the Malvern Mission the first missioner was saying that he was hopeful of building a local congregation among the young people but that he held out little hope of reaching the adults, particularly the men. There have been times when the congregation has increased but even at those times the hardness in response, the difficulty of holding people to faith and church commitment has been recorded.

The forces of oppression, apathy and rebellion were reinforced after the last war. At last the welfare state brought relief from destitution and new housing brought better conditions. But with the welfare state came the benefits system which has done so much to reinforce the taking away of responsibility, of making choices and living with the consequences of actions. The high-rise housing took away from the community life and the open doors of the streets. As people became more affluent and acquired more things, crime increased, the doors began to shut and locks and bolts were added.

Unemployment has again stalked Canning Town in the 1970s and 1980s. Johnny Ringwood, chair of the

Mayflower Council described his three adult sons as the flotsam and jetsam of society with few choices, rejected and thrown on the scrapheap. The London Dockland Development Corporation (LDDC) and the borough council have made great efforts to regenerate the area commercially, socially and environmentally but to date those efforts, partly successful on the Isle of Dogs, have failed here.

Relationships between men and women have been affected. Gordon Barley, Mayflower's present community worker, recently summarized it.

Women on the one hand are expected to be subservient to the man, but on the other hand, have the lion's share of the daily responsibilities for the home and family. Consequently they have to shout to be heard, and tend to be pacified rather than taken seriously and then only as a last resort. Essentially the man wants a quiet life.

He [the provider and head of the household] has for much of the century not been able to be much of either, and has either gone off to war, sea, or closer to home, the pub. Whether intentionally or not, the consequence is the same, which is that he shirks his responsibility and the women become the head of the family . . . His way has in many cases been either to act violently (physically or verbally) towards her or let her take all the decisions.

. . .

Patrick Butler, a resident in the 1980s, whose story is included later, wrote a song called, 'The Sun Goes Down'.

> 1 Fish and chips in front of the T.V.
> Feet up, hard day, ain't been busy
> Kids are outside throwing stones
> Going in boxes pulling out telephones

Chorus
The sun goes down in Canning Town
People hurry home in the evening light
As the sun goes down in Canning Town
I wonder what is going to happen tonight

2 Girls stay at home while the men go boozing
Married to win now they feel they are losing
Mother crying on the fourteenth floor
Dad left home the day before

Chorus
3 Hammers play on a Wednesday night
The lads are up there hoping for a fight
Little old lady mugged in the subway
Someone hears but turns the other way

Chorus
4 But there are smiling faces
and a Spirit that won't be broken
Jesus cares so why deny Him
You're never gonna know unless you try him

Chorus
So let the Sun rise up in Canning Town
Let Him take you home in the morning light
Let the Son rise up in Canning Town
Let Him take you home it will be all right.

Patrick wrote that the song reflects '. . . something of the
pain felt in many lives around Canning Town. When I first
came here I didn't really notice it. "People are used to it,"
I thought. I find now though that the "girls staying at
home" have names and faces, and the men boozing never
really find the peace they look for. Although I've had to
chase away the kids throwing stones so many times, I know
that they are crying out for some real excitement in life —
the sort that Jesus spoke of.'[4]

The loneliness of the high-rise dweller

That is why many people who have come to work at the Centre have felt such pressure. It is not just a culture shock for middle-class staff and residents to come and live in the East End. They come under the same spiritual forces which have caused such devastation in local lives. Marriages, finances, sobriety come under fierce attack. Any latent weakness in any of these areas is exploited to the limit so that at times people have feared for their own and others' sanity.

As the history of the Centre is traced you will see many of these battles being fought out. Christian faith is built on hope — not a vague hope that things can be made a little better, but a hope rooted in God's promises. Exekiel speaks of that sovereign act of God. 'When I demonstrate to the nation the holiness of my great name — the name you disgraced among them — then they will know that I am the Lord. I, the Sovereign Lord, have spoken. I will use you to show the nations that I am holy (Ezekiel 36:23).

·2·

From Malvern Mission to
the Dockland Settlement

(1894-1957)

AT THE END of the last century the feeling of superiority by the middle and upper classes to the 'lower' classes was more openly expressed. There was, however, a desire in a number of public schools for the boys to be made aware of their social responsibilities. Malvern College, a fairly new public school had in 1882 adopted the Parish of All Saints, Haggerston in Hackney, and contributed £80 a year towards providing a parish nurse. They wanted to do more and were anxious to find a really suitable district. Ben Tinton, who was on the staff of the Mission for twenty-five years, describes how the solution came in an unexpected way.

One of the leading daily papers printed a series of articles as to which seemed the worst street in London, and the result of these articles was that Vincent Street, Canning Town, a street in a very neglected area in the East End of London, was voted the worst street. Every effort was made to obtain a house to start in a small way in Vincent Street without success, but a house was obtained in Cooper Street which ran parallel with Vincent Street, and the Malvern College Mission started, a minute beginning destined to grow into a big national movement, and yet originally just a workman's cottage similar to those occupied by the people of the neighbourhood.

A missioner was sent down who occupied two rooms for personal use, one room a club room and one room as a tiny chapel – the effort was an immediate success and it was not long before two adjoining cottages were added to the Mission property, and then, within three years, it was found possible to obtain two houses in that much desired place Vincent Street, where spiritual and moral welfare work amongst the women and girls of the area was commenced. The back yards were linked up and a small corrugated iron church built there, and this was the original Malvern College Mission.[1]

· · ·

The Bishop of Colchester wrote: 'In a parish of 17,000 people there are at present only three clergy; twice that number would certainly be none too many. The district crowded with the tenements of artisans and dock labourers seems to call aloud for some mission work carried out by men of Christian principle and devotion which may elevate and cheer and brighten the laborious and often dreary lives of these toilers.'[2]

The Mission was established in September 1894 with Reverend G. F. Gillett as its first full-time missioner. The College contributed £200 a year. Each term the missioner went to Malvern to talk to the boys about the work of the Mission — the opening of Boys' Clubs, a Working Men's Club, and a Church Lads' Brigade; the holding of Sunday schools; the building of the little church, the work of the Mission nurse who visited and tended the sick. In 1898 he described the ambition of the Mission as being '. . . to carry on the church's work amongst her people from both a religious and a social point of view and to be a centre of religious influence and social good.'[3]

Looking back at what was attempted, it is surprising how many of the modern activities have their echoes in the past. One of these was open air meetings, with the missioner going out with a cross and tow lamps to a different street each night, beginning with a hymn and then going on to speak, at first to an audience that was mainly children then gradually men and women would come out of doors to listen.

Few people give much credit to their predecessors or their successors. Reginald Kennedy Cox who became the driving force behind the work for nearly fifty years said he had been bored by the reports from the missioner while he had been a boy at Malvern. He was an actor and amateur playwright who loved the life of West End theatre. One day he visited the Old Bailey in search of material for a play and saw a youth of nineteen or twenty standing in the dock. The lad had fallen in love with a girl, had to go away on a voyage and on his return found she was going to have a child by another man. He brooded about it for days and after a heavy drinking bout, killed her. He was caught at once and pleaded guilty. Now he was being sentenced to be hanged by the neck until he was dead. Kennedy Cox felt totally crushed and his dramatic efforts utterly unreal and futile in the face of such tragedy. It was the turning point in bringing him down to Canning Town to link with his old school Mission.

He has written about these experiences in a number of books — his autibiography, *The Happiest Man* and *Docklands Saga*. He had an individual style of operating. When he arrived in 1907 the buildings were a shambles — the club rooms being cobbled together by knocking out various walls of the original terraced cottages. There was very little equipment that was not broken. The very roughness of the neighbourhood, the desperate conditions under which people lived, challenged Kennedy Cox. What these men and women, boys and girls lacked most in their daily lives was 'beauty'. They were hungry for it, outwardly and inwardly. Give these people somewhere to meet where beauty, cleanliness, peace were to be found, then the spirit would soon grow and blossom.

Kennedy Cox moved in. 'I dreamt a whole series of new

Queen Mary's visit to the Dockland Settlement, accompanied by Reginald Kennedy Cox.

dreams and then I started out to make them come true.'[4] Clubs were organized separating the adults from the children, the boys from the girls. A football team was formed and his work had begun. The biggest initial problem was how to keep men and women from 'getting drunk and behaving like animals'. So Saturday nights were organized at the Mission with a cine projector and some of the early silent films supplemented by a series of 'vulgar' turns booked from a small music-hall agent. They kept this up until eleven o'clock when the pubs closed in Canning Town, then Kennedy Cox marshalled a small force of helpers, three men and two women to picket the Iron

Bridge and argue, plead or bully the boys and girls who
wanted to cross to get to the Poplar pubs which didn't close
till midnight. They even invaded the first two pubs. They
fought all along the line and the publicans fought them in
turn. Finally at about one o'clock, working in pairs, they
took the drunks home.

They concocted a sort of Sunday evening propaganda as
well. Using a lantern in one of the street windows and
throwing the picture onto the house wall opposite, they
showed any film which had a religious significance supplemented by Church Army slides. From another window
Kennedy Cox shouted out a running commentary on the
slides. Large crowds blocked the street and the final slide
said: 'This is nothing; come inside and see our Sacred Film.'

Kennedy Cox didn't duck the difficult discussions. At the
time of the General Strike in 1926 there was a good deal
of curiosity as to what the attitude of Dockland Settlement
would be. In those days strike pay was usually paid out in
public houses. Kennedy Cox offered the Dockland premises
to the two largest local trade unions, the General Workers'
and the Railwaymen as a centre for distributing pay. They
were provided with committee rooms as well as general
assembly halls and they had telephones and other facilities
with nothing to pay. To remain even-handed, Kennedy Cox
also offered the premises to soldiers who were being sent
into the area to run some of the services and keep order. So
strikers and soldiers were under the same roof. With
thousands of men suddenly finding themselves flung into
the streets with nothing to do and often in an ugly frame
of mind the Settlement threw open all the clubrooms, every
billiard table available, every canteen running with oceans
of tea and coffee and mountains of heavy sweet cakes. They
opened a boxing booth able to hold several hundred men.
All the football grounds were put into use with improvized
league matches and, said Kennedy Cox, '. . . as a final

Machiavellian touch, I continually posted up in prominent places the official telephone bulletins of how the strike was being broken. This has a great effect upon the men.'[5]

A team of staff and helpers was enlisted after the First World War. Captain Ben Tinton came at first to do day work as secretary but one night when there was no one to help in the clubs he offered to stay behind and was very successful. He became Kennedy Cox's second-in-command and took over from him in 1937. Douglas Minton joined in 1919. He had a flair for club work and became director of all the clubs. He had grown up as an orphan at the Queen Victoria Orphanage in Paddington and had taken jobs as a pageboy and hall porter before going to fight for 'King and Country'. Minnie remembered the squalor of those early days: He wrote in 1961:

In the room where I slept I had an umbrella over the bed and buckets on the floor to catch the rain . . . In those days people came here for very different reasons from those which bring them here now – ½d baths on a Saturday morning; daytime clubs for the unemployed to keep them out of trouble and doing boot mending for their children; queuing up for bread and marge and cocoa; Sunday football to keep them out of the pubs after a footballers' service in the chapel. People had nowhere else quite so warm in the winter. On Saturday nights there were, maybe, up to a thousand people here, over half of them old men watching the boxing until the pubs there closed. Others, packing the theatre, the gallery and down stairs, watching silent films and variety turns, others still, dancing.

On my first night in club I was shown into a room full of 9-11-year-old boys. With the door shut a large rat came out of a hole, so I stood on a broken chair and talked to them about the dangers of hanging on the back of coal carts until the rat went back again. On the second night, the girls in the cookery room above dropped a bag of flour through a hole in the ceiling right onto my head as I was passing

below. Boys were made to sit on newspapers as the seats were damp
from the rain.[6]

...

Dorothy Brierley also came at that time and headed the
ladies' side of the work for many years. Miss Oliver a friend
of Kennedy Cox's from his home on the Isle of Wight held
the fort through the First World War and continued for
some years afterwards.

Kennedy Cox had offered to return to the Malvern
Mission after the First World War on condition that he was
in charge, and although he would look to Malvern School
for a certain proportion of the maintenance, beyond that he
would be responsible for everything needed. This was
agreed by the headmaster of Malvern. Kennedy Cox
although recognizing the place would always be a Mission
did not like the title 'missioner' and decided to change the
name to a Settlement. They would not be the Malvern
Settlement as they were not settled in Malvern. As they
were working down by the docks, Dockland seemed right.
So the official title became Dockland Settlement and the
Malvern Clubs, but everyone knew it as 'Docklands'.

Reginald Kennedy Cox set about the entire rebuilding of
the network of clubrooms which had been up till then
improvised out of old and dilapidated Victorian cottages
with the original ghastly wallpaper hanging in strips from
the walls and rat holes everywhere. They had been
demoralizing rooms to work in and on more than one
occasion the ceilings of the boys' clubs had collapsed. To
make matters worse tiny rooms and narrow passages were
serious fire risks.

The new building was done section by section. Mrs
Freeman Cowan gave as a memorial to her son killed in the
war the first large hall, painted grey and subdued blue. This
housed a maze of halls and clubrooms for many different

activities. King George V and Queen Mary were invited to tea to open it.

Then one day a very old little man came to visit the Settlement. It was Bernhard Baron, a great philanthropist. He came to see things for himself, was pleased, then bluntly asked what was wanted. Kennedy Cox commented that when you are dealing with a man who may either be referring to £10 or £10,000 it is a little difficult to know how to answer. Afterwards they found out that he had £12,000 in mind, sufficient to build a large swimming baths. Sadly he did not live to see it opened.

The next addition was a theatre, 'a little building of real beauty where only Shakespeare or opera was played and modern problem plays strongly excluded'.[7] Then there was the roof garden — it had a paved stone terrace with a rose pergola on either side, a sundial in the centre and the inevitable fountain at the end. Fortunately it was just above the smoke zone so there was a splendid view of the docks with their cranes and shipping.

On Sunday afternoons we used to set out a hundred or more deckchairs, and boys could bask away the lazy hour until chapel time and still within them a certain amount of that restless spirit that permeatres East London on Sunday afternoons. But our roof garden was at its best on a summer's night when darkness hides the ugly immediate surroundings. Coloured lights flash out and modern music loses much of its raucous squawk when heard on the soft night air. I have never forgotten the revealing remark of a young girl allowed up for the first time to one of these roof-garden dances. It was a glorious night, and as she flung herself back in a deckchair, she exclaimed to one of our ladies, 'Oh, miss, it's like heaven or' (with an even more rapt expression) 'Brighton!'[8]

...

Two main building efforts remained — the accommodation, or permanent residence, and a new chapel. Everyone on the committee realized that the existing accommodation for staff and resident helpers was in the last stages of decay and collapse, but everyone was not equally enthusiastic about the chapel. Kennedy Cox felt strongly a new chapel would give a sense of proportion to the work in keeping with the beauty of the new and up-to-date clubrooms. All the staff supported this view and were prepared to continue to live in spartan conditions until 'a worthy chapel was an accomplished fact'. Kennedy Cox received strong encouragement from Princess Helena Victoria and it was decided that the chapel would be dedicated to St George for the boys and St Helena for the girls.

The architect Mr Raymond gave Kennedy Cox a remarkably free hand. He wanted a building that would have all the dignity of an ancient building — they took as their model Lincoln's Inn dining hall — with the advantages of a modern one. The chapel has panelling and a beautiful timbered roof. There is a cupola on the roof crowned with a lead weathercock of St George and the Dragon. At the west end there is a glorious cathedral-like stained-glass window by Bell. It is a blaze of colour and embodies the return of the Lord in triumph to the earth. Over the altar is a rose window of scarlet and gold. There were no seats for a choir — Kennedy Cox was insistent that they all do their own singing, but there was a musicians' gallery at each side of the altar. As he could never understand why it was necessary for people to be uncomfortable in church, the seats were padded both at the back and on the seats in a darkish brown canvas. Six of these long seats, now lining the walls, have been recovered this year.

The dedication of the chapel in April 1930 was a magnificent occasion. Twelve hundred people were squeezed into a space that held only eight hundred. Flat against the wall were a hundred of the biggest Scouts and on the opposite wall a hundred of the biggest Guides. The pick of the men in the Docklands Noble Order of Crusaders were in one of the minstrels' galleries and the choir of the Chapel Royal, Savoy were in the other. The band of the Royal Engineers behind the altar, at the front of the altar steps boys from the other Dockland Settlements in Southampton, Bristol, Rotherhithe and Millwall. Princess Helena Victoria was in the chancel. Following bishops in procession came the guest of honour, Her Majesty the Queen.

At almost the same time the money was raised and the two accommodation blocks were built, one for the men on the Vincent Street side of the garden and the other for the women on the Cooper Street side. These were designed with an Oxbridge college quadrangle in mind and each had a black and white mock-tudor façade:

The first essential to finance this growing work was publicity. Kennedy Cox was a genius at this. At ground level they were organizing a mass of clubs, each with a canteen needing different women workers every night of the week. These women on their return to their West End homes would pass the word round interesting others and so the snowball rolled.

Royal patronage was sought and obtained. Kennedy Cox's book is littered with the names of the aristocracy and the Royal Family — King George V and Queen Mary came on more than one occasion. The Duke of York later King George VI presented a football cup and as patron visited year by year, on one occasion ceremoniously demolishing the famous condemned cottage. The Princess Royal and the Duke of Windsor (Edward VIII) visited more than once. In later years Princess Margaret became patron and paid a number of visits and the Duke of Edinburgh came one evening for a boxing match.

Kennedy Cox managed to get Lord Beatty First Lord of the Admiralty and Lord Crewe, British Ambassador in Paris to serve as trustees. Every year a function was organized at the Mansion House provided by the Lord Mayor of London. Each Lord Mayor also visited the Settlement during his year of office. Speakers at these occasions have included the cabinet minister, J.H. Thomas; Sir John Simon, fresh from India; Lord Reading a retiring Viceroy of India; Arthur Henderson another cabinet minister and Lord Baldwin, the then Chancellor of the Exchequer. Thousands of pounds were generated by these dinners.

Tottenham Hotspur and West Ham United both played a series of matches in aid of the work. Spurs also turned their football ground at White Hart Lane into a vast boxing arena on a lovely June night and Kennedy Cox was thrilled to lead Carpentier into the ring, followed by Joe Beckett, Frank Moran and many more boxers. This event achieved a record 'gate' at the ground. Perhaps the biggest effort involved the hiring of the Albert Hall for a whole week for 'The Heart of Empire Ball' at which a huge Empire Pageant Procession was staged under the direction of Nigel Playfair.

Everything that Kennedy Cox organized seemed to be on a grand scale. To raise money for the chapel he went on an extensive tour of the United States and when the new buildings were completed, a jumble sale on a vast scale was held in the West End. This was to become an annual event. It lasted two days and made at least £1,000 every year towards maintaining the work. Dockland Settlements became a national movement. The buildings at Canning Town were called No. 1 and became a model for a total of nine Settlements located in dock areas as far apart as Southampton, Plymouth and Bristol as well as a convalescent home at Herne Bay.

Kennedy Cox was convinced that effective social work must have a firm religious basis. He was determined that boys and girls should have religion as a foundation to build their lives on, a religion utterly simple and also 'blazingly sincere'. His very decided views on services were not popular with the clergy.

He catered for a mass of very different worshippers. Hardened football players grouped together usually in public-house teams were very anxious to have Sunday football but had no ground available. Kennedy Cox provided the ground on the condition they came to a short Football Service before starting the game.

For ordinary club members Sunday services were fitted round late sleeping and eating habits. In the early days he wore himself out by the number of services he had to take or share in on Sundays. He was never at fewer than eight and often it was nine or ten. The original old corrugated chapel collapsed and was replaced by a temporary chapel. This was tiny and as numbers grew they had to duplicate and sometimes triplicate the services. None of the services used to last for more than twenty minutes or half an hour. Kennedy Cox felt it was 'desperately difficult to retain the high emotional tension which the tremendous reality of religion should engender for more than a very brief space of time'.[9] All the clubs were open on Sunday afternoons and there was the canteen with draughts, chess and a mass of comic papers as well as mixed bathing in the swimming pool.

On summer Sundays they hired every available bicycle from the local cycle agents. The boys and girls were sent off in groups with a few adults taking a picnic lunch. Kennedy Cox telephoned for a cheap high tea at the village selected and also sent a letter to the vicar asking either for a special early service or the use of the church. 'The result was that Sunday by Sunday a host of very ordinary healthy boys and girls spent an energetic, clean happy Sunday and began to draw near to a, for them, often very remote God under the pleasantest auspices.'[10]

First Wedding in the Mayflower Church – Mr & Mrs Black – 1930

A number of the older people in Canning Town remember the Dockland Settlement well. Mrs Black, now aged eighty-six, who was the first person to be married in the new chapel in April 1930 still attends Sunday services with her son Ralph. She goes back to Malvern Mission days. 'When I first went there it was only a little hut in the garden and we used to play on the grass. We had dancing on Saturday and needlework on Sunday — Used to go every night before I was married. We had a lot of big people come down . . . The Queen (Queen Mary) came down to see us. That was when the new part was opened.' She remembers her wedding day well. 'Nearly the whole of Canning Town turned out for the new church. The garden wasn't as nice as it is now but it had a big grass field. Now it's lovely.'

For Ralph as a boy, 'It was my lifeline, there and St Luke's, the two places where I was all the time. I was more at

Docklands in my early days. There was nowhere then for us to go anyway. We couldn't afford to go anywhere. What they did have there was the opportunity to join in almost everything. I remember very clearly there was a fish pond in the garden. We were allowed to catch fish round there. I was leaning over and went in and had to come home in Miss Brierley's blazer.' Ralph still mends his own shoes from the skill he learnt at Docklands.

Flo Ham still a regular church attender cooked for the resident medical students for seven years from 1949. Gwen Levett used to dance on the roof garden on the old block with her future husband, Jim. 'Jimmy was a short-time worker even then before the war so we never had a lot of money. We used to have to pay a subscription (to Dockland Settlement) — it wasn't a lot, only a nominal sum. Jimmy used to run the football team round there and play football for them. They had cookery classes — we used to go and make cakes, and throw them out of the window! They used to be hard as bullets! We had lots of fun.'

She remembers when she was a girl being told: 'You should go round the Dockland Settlement to get you off the streets. I think it used to be people from comfortable families that came down and worked from what I can make out. Sort of come to the East End and do some work with poor people . . .'

Ralph Black remembers: 'The number of events going on at the weekend in the garden, outings going out in vans and cars, even down to the hop fields at weekends were a very common feature. I think up to then it was, all come whoever you are, whatever you believe in, whatever you don't believe in. It was for the welfare of the community in my opinion. My dad was a painter and he used to do all sorts of things up there in terms of painting and decorating.'

Steve Boulton who died in 1988 wrote: 'It catered very much for the physical needs of the area. And in a different way the spiritual.

But for the people of that time it served a very real need, and took
us out of a very mundane life.'

• • •

Most of the London Dock area went up in flames during
the Second World War due to the repeated air attacks.
Miraculously the Dockland Settlement buildings were
spared, helped by the efforts of the bursar, Reginald Logan
Hunt and a small band of workers fighting the enemy's
incendiary bombs night after night. Several of the
clubrooms had to be turned into a mortuary after the bomb
hit Hallsville School and the resident workers had the
terrible task of identifying if possible the remains of their
close neighbours. The Settlement had its own ARP Station
First-Aid Post. It was a clearing house for information of
all kinds. The clubrooms were used nightly as rough
dormitories. Once comparative peace had been restored, an
enormous clothing centre, 'Bundles for Britain', was
organized to distribute a quarter of a million articles. All the
senior youths were fighting in the services; the girls mainly
worked in factories; the women and children were
evacuated, so the old system of crowded nightly clubs died
a natural death. The resident hostels were depleted of social
workers and the government took over the men's hostel for
imported Irish labourers who worked as demolition gangs.
The women's hostel became billets for army officers and
others concerned in restoring the damaged docks.

The war left Dockland Settlement in a sorry state. The
building had deteriorated badly and they had run into debt.
Kennedy Cox came out of retirement to take over on a
temporary basis and pull it together. He had Miss Oliver,
Miss Truscott and Douglas Minton to help him. The whole
site is built on small islands in the marshes intersected by
subterranean streams of water from the docks. The impact
of the heavy German bombs diverted these streams and the

result was that the chapel and the men's hostels began to slide and crack. Large sums of money were needed to underpin the fabric.

A series of wardens was appointed in the following ten years including Harold Kimberley from No. 2 who died of a brain tumour in 1953. David Gardner was appointed chaplain in 1955. Although the work began again on similar lines the climate changed. The gymnasiusm no longer had an appeal, there were far fewer football teams, much more demand for 'modern' dancing. The welfare state and jobs had eliminated much of the 1930s' poverty. There was now the problem of '. . . that cancerous apathy and gross materialism of the mind, engendered so much by the size of the pay packet.'[11] By 1956 it was decided that Dockland No. 1 would have to be closed. Plans were drawn up to dispose of the whole site for commercial purposes and an offer was made.

Into this situation stepped the committee put together by Hugh Gough, the Bishop of Barking, and David Sheppard. Negotiations took place with the Dockland Settlement committee about the bank overdraft, the buildings and future policy. The only commitment Sir Reginald Kennedy Cox wanted was that social clubs should be carried on in a real sense and not as excuses for 'mass conversion'. Agreement was reached and an announcement made in June 1957 confirming that the new committee were taking over. The name was to be Dockland Family Centre and David Sheppard would be the warden.

Clubs closed and preparations were made for a new work to begin. It was daunting. Estimates for capital repair costs ranged around £37,000 — running expensess were estimated between £7,000 and £15,000. Some staff were staying — Rev. David Gardner, Douglas Minton, Margaret Fish and Miss Truscott — but they needed leaders for the girls' and boys' work as Minnie (Douglas Minton) was near retirement. It was agreed that resident staff who had any personal responsibility for the work would be Christian but that hostel and domestic staff need not be Christians. Jean Lodge Patch was appointed as a girls' club leader. It was agreed that grants could be obtained to fund particular salaries. There was some discussion as to whether appeals for money should be made and it was decided that there should be no kind of begging but information would be given on finances to stimulate Christian people to pray. David Sheppard in particular felt that more should be given towards the work by Canning Town itself.

The Dockland Settlement committee then asked if the word Dockland could be dropped from the new name to avoid confusion between the two organizations. No local name seemed to have an authentic ring of Christian adventure about it. Steve Boulton wrote. 'Above the buildings was a model of a ship sailing into the sunset — the Dockland Settlement logo. At a members' meeting in our shabby old buildings we decided to call it Mayflower.'[12]

A Voice in the Wilderness
David Gardner's Story

The transition from Dockland to Mayflower really begins with the appointment of David Gardner as chaplain in 1955 by the Bishop of Barking, Hugh Gough. There was still much war damage. To get to the buildings David travelled by tube and bus to the Barking Road. He then picked his way across a vast bomb site littered with rubbish, paper, bits and pieces of rotting and mouldy furniture to get to the entrance on Cooper Street, a very old and dingy street. The walls of the Settlement's buildings on that side including the chapel were covered with graffiti and there were a number of little niches or grottoes with religious plaques and statues. Not far away was Rathbone Street with its famous

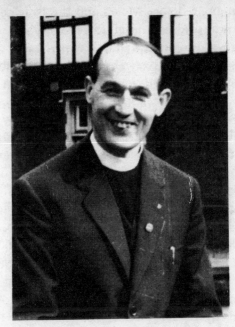

David Gardner – Chaplain 1955-1959

street market. Mrs Olley's jellied eel- and hot-pie stall was right on the corner of it. Mrs Olley, one of only a handful of regular attenders at the 8.30 a.m. Communion Service in the chapel would thrust a hot pie into David's hand every time he passed. 'That's for you, love.'

Hugh Gough, the bishop, was very disturbed about what was going on at the Settlement and even described it as 'the seat of Satan'. He had been pressed to appoint a full-time chaplain and had decided it must be an evangelical. At the large induction service he said forthrightly, 'David Gardner is an evangelical — therefore he will not be wearing vestments, of course.' His support for David during the next months was critical.

On the day of the Induction Service David received a letter with a text from Exodus 23:20–32. It spoke of God sending an angel before Moses and the Israelites through the wilderness to drive out all the enemies that were then occupying the Promised Land. The particular verses that David was to read and reread as God's promise to him over the next few years were 'I will not drive them out from before thee in one year; lest the land become desolate and the beasts of the field multiply against thee. By little and little I will drive them out from before thee until thou be increased and inherit the land. Thou shalt make no covenant with them or with their gods.' There were a number of battles over the next months.

It was inevitable that David's strong evangelical stance would clash with the very Anglo-Catholic practices which had been developed at the Settlement. This led in particular to hostility with the then warden and with Douglas Minton who had been leading the boys' work since 1920. In particular, over the first few weeks there was a running battle between David and Minnie over the placing of the bread, wine and prayer book on the Communion table, David putting them at the left-hand (north) end of the table on Saturday evening and finding them moved to the centre (east) position on Sunday mornings. David remembers Douglas Minton stamping his way along the pavement on his way to the club, and passing under David's window, muttering 'wretched man, wretched man'. Isolated, David felt there was 'not one true believer' in the whole of the Settlement staff and certainly not amongst the club leaders who were also classed as social workers.

But there were encouragements for David. Before he went to Canning Town, a docker came up to him and said, 'We dockers don't want the kind of parson who goes into the pub and drinks and smokes with us. We want the kind of parson who knows what he stands for so that we can go to him when we need him. That does not mean that we will go to him but that is the kind of man we want . . .'

It was when the large doors in Vincent Street leading to the clubrooms were opened and hundreds of young people between eleven and twenty-two-years-old poured into the building on David's first visit that his heart was touched. There was no one to care for their souls or for their eternal welfare. He was conscious of being given a tremendous responsibility.

Gang warfare was rife in the area and it frequently happened that when the premises were packed with young people, as quick as lightning they could empty. A gang fight had broken out somewhere outside and at a given signal, impossible to detect, everybody flooded out of the premises to watch and sometimes take part in it.

David was quickly taught that although they respected their club leaders to some extent, it was never wise when moving about amongst them to have any of them behind his back. Widespread truancy from school was a common feature of the area. One teenage girl coming into the Senior Girls' Club one night boasted she had been to school that day and nobody recognized her.

Douglas Minton asked David to go to the local juvenile court with him one day. Three of the Junior Club boys had been caught by the police breaking into some premises and they were to appear before the local magistrate. The case went against the boys. The magistrate was deliberating with the clerk of the court as to what to do when suddenly Douglas Minton sprang up and said, 'We have got a new padre. He will make himself responsible for these boys and see that this does not happen again.' The offer was accepted on the spot.

As Douglas Minton and the boys came out of the court David said: 'I want you all to come to the Cooper Street entrance at 4 o'clock this afternoon and I will show you how to give your hearts to Jesus.' 'Yes, sir. We'll be there,' the boys promised. At 4 o'clock David was detained for a few minutes in the club rooms on the opposite side of the central courtyard from the Cooper Street entrance. As he made his way to the entrance he saw the boys already in the courtyard. 'How did you boys get in here?' he asked. 'We broke in, sir.' 'You what?' 'We broke in, sir.' 'But don't you realize that was the very thing that caused you to finish up in the magistrates' court?' 'We know, sir. But we came to the Cooper Street door at 4 o'clock and rang the bell and nobody answered. We rang the bell again and nobody answered. So because you said you wanted to tell us how to give our hearts to Jesus we broke in.' Those three boys eventually became the nucleus of the Sunday afternoon Covenanter Bible Class.

This group of thirteen to fifteen-year-olds were given basic Bible teaching each week. Some of the lads later formed themselves into a boys' prayer group who regularly met for prayer together in the side chapel on Saturday mornings. It was a great inspiration to hear them pray quite spontaneously each Saturday morning. Later when some of them were converted they all went missing one Sunday afternoon. When David next saw them he asked where they had been. They told him, 'Down in Southend, sir — witnessing for Jesus to people on the beaches.' One of them, John Peters, was quite fiercely persecuted for his faith by his schoolmates and by neighbours in Liverpool Road, but he would not be put off and became an outstanding and fearless witness for Jesus.

David was also reaching adults. Tom Ham, a crane driver from the docks and his wife, Flo, who cooked at the Dockland, were told by their son who attended Sunday school that David had said they both had to come to the Mothering Sunday service. From that Sunday onwards they were always there. One Sunday there was a howling gale blowing outside and Tom and David stood talking just outside the main chapel doors at the end of a service.

Suddenly a huge gust of wind slammed the heavy doors shut on David's hand, crushing his thumb. David said, 'Bless my soul,' withdrew his hand, tucked it under his arm and went on talking to Tom. Tom said, 'Padre, do you realize what you have done?' He pointed to the bloodstains all down David's white surplice. Describing the incident Tom said he would have said something if *his* thumb had been involved, and it certainly wouldn't have been 'bless my soul'. 'There must be something in this Christianity,' he said, and later committed his own life to the Lord.

So David's ministry was bearing fruit. He still felt on his own as far as the Christian witness, preaching and teaching was concerned, but he still had that promise of God that little by little the enemy forces would be driven out and he would inherit the land.

The cost of running the Centre was presenting a major challenge to the governing body. The money raised by theatre and cinema premieres, by balls at the Dorchester and by Mansion House dinners began to dry up and the staff of social workers and secular club leaders eventually had to go. There were in residence at that time a number of medical students, who by paying rent for their rooms, contributed towards the Settlement's expenses but who caused a lot of problems by their behaviour. One Saturday night they got hopelessly drunk and turned their rooms more or less into brothels. There was a police raid and they were all asked to leave forthwith.

Then, quite unexpectedly, David had a telephone call from someone at the West Ham local authority suggesting the empty rooms be used by Christian teachers who would like to work in the local schools. Very soon some Queen Mary College Christian Union members and a group from a ladies' Bible college in Oxford were moving in. Then a telephone call from the Bishop of Chelmsford suggested that a young ordinand, Malcolm Widdecombe, would benefit from spending a year with David at the Dockland Settlement. Malcolm, straight from Capernwray Hall, was an ardent and lively evangelist and David used him straightaway to give evangelistic talks at the Sunday morning children's service and also to the boy Covenanters. He also spent a lot of time every weekday evening in Douglas Minton's eleven-to-fifteen-year-old boys' club, witnessing amongst them.

David said to the Bishop of Barking, 'We could appoint a staff of Christian workers and club leaders here if only we had the money to pay them.' Just after that the editor of the *English Churchman* newspaper invited David to write an article on his work in the East End. To David's surprise he put it on the front page under a banner headline and himself printed an appeal for funds at the foot of the article. The first response came from an old Malvernian with a cheque for £500. 'I find that my bank balance has swollen more than it ought to have done,' he wrote. 'I want to reduce it by sending this cheque for your Christian workers' fund. Please don't waste time writing to thank me, there are far more important things in life to do than that.' Many more letters followed with cheques for the fund.

The money enabled Christian workers to be employed. Margaret Fish came as lady worker taking over the responsibility for the mums' and other ladies' clubs and for helping in the children's church on Sunday mornings. Tony Dines arrived and did much work in the Senior Boys' Club. John Lywood and Owen Jones came, the latter visiting all the homes in Vincent Street, Cooper Street and the adjacent roads. Richard Thomson, another old Malvernian, then an army captain, now vicar of St Mary's Reigate, became a firm friend and visited frequently at weekends.

Now that they had the Christian people to run it, David had the vision for a Christian bookstall in Rathbone Street. He got in touch with CLC and obtained a supply of books and Bibles on sale or return. Permission was granted by the market authorities and every Saturday the stall was set up. To David's amazement it was the black leather-covered Authorized Version Bibles that the East End people were going for, not the Christian books.

Prayer was fundamental to David's approach. The staff had been praying after breakfast every morning in the side chapel, but with the increasing activities it was decided that in addition they should begin to hold all-night prayer meetings on the first Friday night of every month. The staff at the Bethnal Green Mission were experiencing some difficulties and asked if they might join. David Sheppard writing on David Gardner's departure in 1959 said, 'If ever a work could be said to be rooted in prayer, it is the Mayflower, and this is mainly David's doing.'

A mission was held in the area on the initiative of the principal of St Michael's House, Oxford, a women's Bible and training college to give experience in witnesssing for Christ in the East End and amongst Dockland club members. They visited many homes and streets and held meetings for children, young people and mums. For David it was like a breath of fresh air and he was sorry to see them go. Not so Douglas Minton who growled, 'Now we can get back to normal.' To which David replied, 'Mr Minton, we haven't reached normal yet.'

It was at this stage that David felt increasing pressure from the warden. He made accusations to the bishop that David had not been appearing at the youth clubs during the evening and had totally changed the churchmanship of the Settlement. When the bishop visited the Settlement the warden suggested that David be replaced by an ordained man whom he had been in contact with. Instead of agreeing, the bishop got in touch with the chairman of the Settlement governing body and shortly after that the warden was dismissed.

Another great change was in Douglas Minton. Although David never heard his testimony it became clear that he had been well and truly converted and was speaking about Jesus to anyone he met out in the streets, in Rathbone Market and in his Junior Boys' Club where he could be seen surrounded by a group of boys in an evening helping them to read a chapter of the Bible. David speaks of the great affection Minnie showed him after his conversion.

Douglas Minton was one of the staff members to continue during Mayflower days. He left in 1961, worked for six years at Shoreditch before moving to Elmstead Market and finally Clacton. He was still going strong at ninety when some children from Mayflower were taken there on holiday and he asked them if they knew about the Lord Jesus Christ.

David felt that God was indicating that he should now be working towards a complete takeover of the Centre for the Lord in fulfilment of the Exodus 23 promise. But it was a period of great strain. He felt at times that he was being 'kept an eye on' by some in residence who were reporting back to members of the governing body unhappy at the turn of events. He knew God was doing something but he did not know exactly what. It was a long, anxious, drawn-out period in which God seemed to be saying, 'Wait, Wait, Just wait on me.'

Into this situation came David Sheppard. He contacted David to say certain people had been approaching him about training Christian youth leaders to man some of the youth clubs around the country and that he had been looking for a centre in a down-town area where he could bring this idea into being.

David Sheppard asked, 'What are the chances of taking it over?' To which David Gardner replied, 'You had better go and see the Bishop of Barking. I have already told him that we are very near the stage when we could take it over for the Lord.'

The resulting negotiations led to the setting up of a new governing body entirely composed of committed Christians under the chairmanship of Hugh Gough, the Bishop of Barking, the withdrawal of Princess Margaret as patron and the appointment of David Sheppard as warden with David Gardner being asked to continue as chaplain.

For David this was the complete and miraculous fulfilment of all the promises God had made in that Exodus 23 passage of Scripture. God had sent his angel before. He had kept David in the way. He was now bringing His people into the place He had prepared. This was what David had been working towards. The opposition hadn't been driven out in a year but by little and little until the Christians had increased and were ready to 'inherit the land'.

There is a sadness in the remaining two years of David's stay. Perhaps it was similar to John the Baptist who, having had to break up the hard ground and prepare the way for Jesus's coming had some doubts about the effectiveness of the one he made way for. David's job had been accomplished with the establishment of Mayflower. Over the following months with the recruitment of new staff, especially George Burton, he felt increasingly sidelined and not needed. He finally left in July 1959.

Drawn by the Holy Spirit
Mary Watts's Story

The Dockland Settlement was still called the Malvern Mission by Mary Watts's family and relatives when she was a child. Her mother was a cleaner for the Dockland Settlement so her small feet tapped along the polished floors of the corridors when she was only a toddler, and early memories of Miss Brierley's magnificent painted red fingernails stay in her mind. In the war years she remembers too Red Cross parcels from America that caused much excitement, especially when they sometimes contained colour-print books of fairy tales for the children.

She recalls the wax polish smell of the shiny corridors that led off to small quaint bedrooms with sloping ceilings and leaded diamond-shaped windows which later in the 1950s and '60s were to house a brave band of residents.

'Sunday mornings, I sat in the front pew with what I think were the only adults to attend. Mrs Olley and Mrs Lillywhite.' Mrs Olley owned the pie 'n' mash shop. She stood on a box behind the counter to help her reach to serve you with one penny worth of liquor and mashed potato (liquor is parsley sauce/gravy). After church she served tea from an enamel pot which was about a third of her height and she swirled the tea leaves about with great vigour; the inside of the pot was laden with tartar of church tea throughout the year!!

Mary Watts

'Mrs Olley and my mother were great friends as they were both cleaners at Dockland. Mum didn't attend church in those days. She thought they were all hypocrites. It was her job to throw away the empty whisky bottles, and besides, she had once entered a room to clean it and found the vicar kissing Miss Brierley (just like the TV).

'Mrs Lillywhite had a fine voice, knew all the hymns and I loved to sing along with her. When the service was over I had a sticky picture to lick and put in a book. Once a month there was a parade through the streets with stops at the little shrines (usually in the middle of the street) in memory of those who had fallen in the war. With a shrill blast of the trumpet, a bang on the drum we were off to the next street and back home in time for Sunday lunch . . .

'After the war came Club Night with Miss Trustcot and Mr Minton. Mostly for girls this would mean needlework and drawing (the latter which I loved). I learnt to swim in the pool, encouraged by Miss Trustcot and a determination to take my feet off the bottom even if it meant drowning. Games like netball were held in the large club room upstairs with our boos and screams resounding off the tiled walls.

'Camping at Broxbourne with Mr Minton meant a very small child pulling and dragging her suitcase along the footpath of the river Lea. The suitcase didn't have much in the way of extra clothing but you took your own sheets and pillowcases, towels and blanket, which smelt of the air-raid shelter, and, of course, sandwiches. My chief memories of camp are of creaky, dirty bunk beds and lots of spiders; playing in gravel pits (must have been very dangerous); paddling in the river and being amazed at the sight of dragonflies that colourfully dazzled as they darted above our heads. 'My mother, who had volunteered to help with the cooking, has a big row with Mr Minton. She called him a 'greedy old sod' because he had ate the extra food rations!! Later in life I was to remonstrate with my mother when explaining he had now become a Christian!!

'Later, when I was fourteen years old and feeling very lost inside, I sat on the brick wall that surrounds the maisonettes facing the church door. With a deep longing and yearning for God inside me,

I dared to push open the door and go in. This was about 1953; David Gardner had just arrived. I felt rather shy and inadequate and was not sure how to explain myself . . .

'But the Holy Spirit had me in his sights and three years later, with a sense of inevitabiilty, I returned to Mayflower and committed my life to Christ.'

A scene during a Christmas Party for 3-5-year-olds. December 1959

Mayflower:
the Adventure Begins

(1958–1969)

MAYFLOWER FAMILY CENTRE was incorporated in January 1958. Its object was 'the advancement of the Christian religion by all means and in particular by the encouragement of religious thought and manner of living on the common basis of Christian Fellowship.' David Sheppard was licensed and moved in the same month, the clubs opened in March and a new chapter began.

A vision rarely comes as a ready-made formula dropped into a situation. It emerges as experience and issues are faced and discussed and as God speaks and guides. David Sheppard had encountered at St Mary's Islington, where he was curate, the inappropriateness and irrelevance of some of the approaches used by existing Christian youth organizations like Crusaders, Covenanters, Scripture Union, the Boys' Brigade, Christian Endeavour when face to face with disadvantaged young people in deprived urban areas. More than that, he had felt that the Christian gospel had always been presented by 'outsiders' who had travelled in to tell local people about it or who had come to live for a few years in the district while they were young and single. What was needed were people prepared to live for a long time as neighbours and a place which would be a bridge of neutral ground where meeting and friendship could develop, where young men and women who wanted to serve God with their lives would be able to come and live in an industrial area. They would then see some of its needs, share in Christian work, understand what abilities they had and go away and tackle similar or maybe quite different needs elsewhere.

So the vision and aims took shape. David Sheppard handed a summary to the second and third wardens.

The object has always been:

1 to help an indigenous church develop in the district with local Christian leaders, local Christian homes.

2 to serve the district in the name of Christ, trying to meet some of the social and educational needs of Canning Town.

3 to provide a training ground, though not in any formal sense of training, for Christians (generally from other social backgrounds) who want to learn something about Christian work in areas like this.

Of these objects it was emphasized that first and foremost God had called those at Mayflower to build a church in Canning Town.

Brian Seaman remembers his first visit in the summer of 1958 as a student seven years before he came as full-time chaplain to the Centre.

The Mayflower was quite new then. David Sheppard and the team were still settling down. David Gardener (chaplain or 'padre') and 'Minnie' Minton (youth leader) were still there, having worked for many years previously in the Dockland Settlement. There was a considerable stress on the fact that the Mayflower was quite distinct and different from the Dockland Settlement. It was more than a new name. It included serving the local community and its needs, but now the emphasis was on enabling local people themselves to meet their own needs - material and spiritual - in a truly indigenous church. Mayflower leaders were still imported, but only for as long as it took for the local church to emerge, equipped by the Holy Spirit for responsible leadership and ministry in the area. It was a vision that would mature slowly; certainly for the foreseeable future it would not be a takeover of local people but rather a partnership in which they would serve alongside the imported team. One of the first books recommended to me was Roland Allen's *Missionary Methods - St Paul's or Ours?* I think all the new team had read it and carried it with their Bibles! If the first converts are taught to depend upon the missionary, if all work, evangelistic, educational, social is concentrated in his hands, the infant community learns to rest passively upon the man from whom they receive their first insight into the gospel. Their faith having no sphere for its growth and development lies dormant. A tradition very rapidly grows up that nothing can be done without the authority and guidance of the missionary, the people wait for him to move, and the longer they do so, the more incapable they become of any independent action.[1]

The first and most striking difference between his (St Paul's) action and ours is that he founded 'churches' whilst we found 'Missions'. The establishment of Missions is a peculiarity of our modern methods . . . they have not proved themselves in practice to be very convenient or effective instruments for creating indigenous churches.[2]

I was very impressed with the Christian commitment of the team which came together under David Sheppard's ('Skipper's') leadership as I gradually got to know them. After my first spell during the summer of 1958 I used to make return visits, enjoying both the occasional game of cricket - in the best company! - and the excitement and stimulus of a new work of God growing. I was soon under the spell of George Burton the new Senior Youth Leader who became Skipper's right-hand man. They were as different as the proverbial chalk and cheese. George had no interest whatsoever in cricket! I think he saw it as the refined activity of the privileged middle classes - or something like that - suitable for educated young Englishmen with culture and good manners. But the partnership between Skipper and George was electrifying. Here were two men from completely different backgrounds united in their commitment to Jesus Christ and in their vision of an indigenous church of Canning Town people.

To quote George's own words: 'Like the scaffolding which is essential while a building is under construction but which only gets in the way once the work is finished, so the Christians from outside who have helped at the start should be prepared to move into the background as local people become available to take their place.'[3]

. . .

There was a lot of excitement as the work began. Brian Seaman remembers travelling with George Burton in his car, stopping and engaging someone in conversation about his or her soul. 'As far as I know it was usually a complete stranger. I guess it must have been like that for the first few disciples of Jesus as they watched and listened to Him seeking and saving the lost. Indeed a lot of what went on in those early days at Mayflower seemed to me to be taken straight out of the pages of the gospels. Rosemary Finch remembers:

It was exciting. You would be working in the clubhouse and you felt it needed a coat of paint. I remember when we did the girls' room up over there. We didn't have anything. I remember praying with George and a few others. We prayed for paint and it came in. We prayed for hair dryers and somebody rang up and we got a load of hair dryers! It was quite amazing how some things particularly in the early days used to happen. It was almost like Mueller must have felt in his day. There was excitement about it . . .

. . .

Many of those early principles became fundamental in people's lives. Rosemary reflects:

I would say that Mayflower probably had the most significant impact on my Christian life. Lots of the things I've learnt through Mayflower I've put into practice. It was drilled into me – T, L, U, – you must give people time, you must give people love, you must give them understanding. The need to be non-judgmental, not prejudiced, and I've sort of built my life on those principles. The thing I learnt very early on at Mayflower is the need to have a vision. Without a vision the people perish. I had a vision because I felt God had called me to work in the inner city and now that I've moved out to the country I feel that God has given me a vision for the villages. You felt that you were actually working together for a corporate vision which was to preach the gospel, to bring people to Jesus Christ to a living faith, and also for them to take over in leadership.

• • •

The scaffolding needed to be there and was provided by the staff and helpers or 'residents'. Staff strength and support was very important and the staff meeting had a high priority. Weekly meetings would be from 9 a.m. to 3 p.m. with a break for lunch. Bible study was an important element. Rosemary Finch remembers:

That was tremendous for working together as a team. Learning – having your corners rubbed off. Submitting to one another in terms of thinking through ideas that maybe other people didn't see. If somebody was down there was always somebody up on the team to give support. You saw the work as a whole. You had the same vision and therefore there was unity.'

Grace Sheppard writes, 'One of the most positive things for me was when David invited the wives of the two clergy to be full members of the staff meeting. Having lost a good deal of self-confidence during my breakdown, it did wonders for my dignity and rehabilitation to be part of the action in this way, and to be allowed to take responsibility for pieces of work in the Centre.

• • •

The pressure of working in Canning Town was recognized. Keeping Christian workers fresh in their work was important. There were too many examples of men and women who were broken or depressed or who left just when their most useful work might be done. Staff were to have a weekly day off which was regarded as sacrosanct, there was six weeks' holiday during the year, preferably with three being taken together in the summer and each staff member was entitled to a 'furlough' or long leave of between three and six months every three to four years to be used as the staff member wished. David Sheppard had nine months in Australia in 1962/3 linked with the England winter cricket tour, staying on in Sydney to speak at a number of meetings.

In addition to the staff there was an army of part-time voluntary helpers — up to twenty-four being in residence at any one time. Initially many were attracted by the drawing power of David Sheppard. He knew that he was a 'marketable commodity' and deliberately set out to attract young people to the Mayflower for training. George Burton was also someone people wanted to work with. People were in particular attracted to working in the youth club in an inner-city area. Many other voluntary helpers travelled down from central London to help one night a week in the clubs.

Residents had a great deal going for them. They were young and so the right age to work with teenagers. They had time to give and no family responsibilities. Many had talent and one or two were very gifted. They had much goodwill and a great deal of idealistic drive. The majority also had behind them an education and background that encouraged them to experience cultures other than their own. What residents lacked, in all but a few exceptional cases, were expertise and experience.

Residents came for different reasons — some to serve God

and man, some for training and experience, some to fill in time before starting training, usually for ordination. This was the third part of the original aims of Mayflower — bringing Christians from other social backgrounds to learn about Christian work in the inner city. Generally speaking the experience was very worthwhile. Tony McCutcheon put together the responses of two hundred past and present residents and staff from 1958 to 1981. His assessment was:

That it was an outstanding experience for most, costing much and rewarding more. That being part of a team committed to serving Jesus and others in practical involvement made it a unique corporate experiences different in kind from almost all other training experience. The depth of fellowship sprang from the depth of commitment to God, the Mayflower and each other. The fun and laughter were a direct by-product of shared work and achievement by people who were enhanced by the meaningful work that was demanded from them.'

...

Did the experience at Mayflower help towards ordained ministry? The responses from the survey were over-whelmingly positive. People spoke of subsequent ministry in inner-city Manchester, a downtown parish in Gloucester, youth work in Cardiff, parish work in Shoreditch and life in Santiago, Chile. All spoke of the insights and lessons learnt in their time at Mayflower.

There was also criticism, and some real hurt, but in particular the challenge to shed middle-class appearance values was seen as a real contribution to honesty and growth.

Some of the tensions of the different goals were apparent even at this early stage. If the emphasis was to be on developing the local church then looking after and supporting residents could not be a high priority in staff time and residents could often feel neglected. The staff had a very strong mutually supportive network, the residents did not. There was sometimes a feeling of us and them between staff and residents perhaps highlighted by George Burton's often aggressive attitude towards middle–class residents. There was also staff protectiveness towards local church members which meant that residents were not given the opportunity to make close friendships with local people though some did manage to do this. This led to a sense of isolation accentuated by the hostel experience where residents lived with other residents and local people were not in general allowed in. The scaffolding was separate from the main building though it did provide good support and felt a real sense of purpose in doing so.

One other tension in those days was financial. The cost of repairing and refurbishing the maze of buildings had crippled Dockland Settlement. Mayflower had secured grant money for initial repairs and improvements but the ongoing staff and running costs were high. The Mayflower Council minute book is studded with references to the need for a high occupancy rate in the hostel in order to stay solvent. Residents paid rent and the money was needed to balance the books. Tony McCutcheon commented that, '. . . the emphasis on quantity has sometimes led to acceptance of residents of low standard.'

There was a lot of discussion about culture and morality. Brian Seaman writes:

Every culture has its beliefs and ways of doing things, and these years found us grappling with the whole relationship of Christianity to its surrounding culture. Christianity is not identified with respectable middle-class ways; neither is it identified with working-class ways. It informs, challenges both. Mayflower, with its heavy emphasis on an indigenous church of the area, was built on the conviction that to be a Christian and a Christian leader you didn't have to be a well-educated, correct-speaking, well-dressed resident of suburbia. All our efforts went into affirming the local Canning Town culture, not judging it. Key phrases were 'unjudging friendship' and 'accepting people as they are'. I bought this, and still believe it is an important insight into God's mercy and love towards us sinners – e.g. the prodigal son's father in his welcome of his returning son. However, I can also see the dangers. In our efforts to affirm local people and their culture it seemed sometimes as if they could do no wrong. The call to repentance and a new life in Christ seemed sometimes to be muted.

. . .

George Burton, a man from a working-class background himself, wanted to highlight the positives of a working-class culture. He described them as people who are generally friendly, quick-witted and hospitable — they are quick to rally round when someone is ill or in trouble. Because they have been thrown together with other people, they develop a group instinct in marked contrast to the pronounced individualism of people from a middle-class background. They are ill at ease when separated from their group and are happiest wherever there is noise and activity even if they are not in the mood to take an active part themselves. He was quick to see any sham and hypocrisy.

There was also a real concern that new Christians would lose their working classness. David Sheppard wrote in 1962:

We believe that the real challenge of Christian service is here. We do not therefore at present encourage our Christians to go off to train for the ministry or the overseas mission field or for club leadership. We urgently need a 'first generation' of Christians working out their faith in ordinary jobs and not as 'professional Christians'. When they have won through in their own environment and in an ordinary job and have proved Christ's power here and when the foundation of a local church is established, we expect to see God call some away to all these forms of 'full-time service'. But at present this seems to me evasion of His real call to service, escape from the hardest problems of living the Christian life, and dissipation of Christian beginnings which could grow into a strong Church.

Coupled with this was a concern that people would move out of the area. He wrote:

We are concerned at how easy it is for young Christians from a working-class background to change themselves socially by imitation of Christians from other social groups. This normally seems to cause them to have less and less contact and sympathy with their neighbours, and when they marry they usually move out of the district to an area which is middle class – and where the church is very often much stronger. We believe God has called us to build a church which may be described truly as indigenous to Canning Town just as much as if we were working in India or Africa.[4]

. . .

George Burton if anything was even stronger.

From the earliest days of the Sunday Group I have shielded the members from the influence of outsiders. Visitors from outside only came in on rare occasions after careful briefing. I wanted to encourage the group to grow up naturally. They would be sure to copy those adults whom they saw, and this involved the danger of their becoming so different from their own people that they would be poor tools for spreading the gospel among them. If someone were to come and talk to them of classical music, they would become interested in this kind of music, forsaking and perhaps even despising the pop music that is current in their circles. If someone were to talk about the glories of Army life, they may want to leave the area and join the Army. But we believe that God is calling us to challenge these young Christians to remain in Canning Town and build their homes here. Therefore we want them to keep their natural characteristics and habits so that they can be better ambassadors for Christ to their own people. God may call some of them away, but we do not want them automatically to drift away as happens with so many people converted from this sort of district.[5]

...

Janet and Jim Gosling remember. 'The vision also included encouraging young newly married Christian couples to stay within the locality in order to witness alongside others of similar backgrounds by purchasing houses for them to live in at a reasonable rent, thus saving the need to perhaps look further afield. Mayflower Housing Association was established for that purpose. It enabled us to make our first home in Plaistow, not far from Mayflower.'

Brian Seaman writes of the progress of the work at that time.

Meanwhile the Lord added to our number those who were being saved – perhaps not 'daily' but steadily. Youngsters were being brought to Christ through the youth work, with the Sunday Group leaders growing in maturity. Adults were coming to faith through adult activities. Every autumn we ran a 'Searching Group' to which adults whom we had contacted in various ways were invited to think through the basics of the Christian faith together. We realized the importance of the group for learning in a culture where generally speaking individuals didn't read books and where people thought and acted together rather than as individuals. Although this came as a new insight to me at the time it is not surprising when you consider that the vast majority of those who came to the groups were part of a close group on the shop floor and lived closely together in rows of terraced houses or blocks of flats. There was strength and solidarity in the group and defence against exploitation. So it wasn't altogether surprising that people were converted as a group. What's good enough for him is good enough for me.

With my evangelical background I was a bit wary of this. I had been taught that people came to Christ one by one as individuals; you couldn't come in on someone else's ticket. But when I looked

again at the New Testament – which I was constantly urged to do
– I saw that sometimes whole families believed together (e.g. Lydia's
and the Philippians' jailer's families: Acts 16:15,34. At Jonah's
preaching a whole city repented: Jonah 3:5).

● ● ●

The achievements of that period were very significant. In
a survey of *West Ham Church Life 1984* the writers comment:
'The achievement of the earlier period is unique in that there
are hardly any white male Christians born and brought up
in Canning Town of that generation to be found in the
churches of South West Ham who did not come to faith
through the Mayflower. In addition the role of the
Mayflower in training many of the professional Christians
involved in urban mission and church work in different
parts of the country is of immense significance.'[6]

The Mayflower was earning a reputation far wider than
Canning Town. The *Log of the Mayflower* gave news of the
work to over five thousand supporters around the country.
David Sheppard as a nationally known cricketer attracted
a lot of publicity. News reporters, journalists, photo-
graphers and others descended on the place. Grace Sheppard
writes:

We invited many visitors to come and see and hear what was
happening. We acknowledged our need of friends. We needed their
interest, their prayers, and their money. Each month we held an 'At
Home' in the main club room with refreshments. There was a brief
introductory talk about our aims with time for questions, a tour of
the premises and the chance to talk with local people. Together with
the monthly newsletter, called the *Log of the Mayflower*, this
constituted a real bridge with the outside world, and helped us
towards a Christian interdependence where we could both give and
receive to and from the wider church and community.

● ● ●

How far was the vision being achieved? Local people were becoming deeply involved in leading and helping the children's and young teen's work, both on Sundays and in the club. Jim Gosling and Ted Lyons (both later ordained) took a month off work to go on a course at the London College of Divinity to help them with their Lay Reader's exams. Local people began to experience life beyond Canning Town. Alan Dennis remembers: 'for the first time ever I went away for weekends — I went somewhere other than Canning Town. I'd hardly ever been out of round here. To go away weekends and go abroad. Typical Mayflower outings. So from that point of view my horizons widened incredibly. I think God had a plan for us when I look back. That was all part of what I had to learn.'

Jim and Janet Gosling remember there was a request from John Pearce of St Paul's Homerton for someone from Mayflower to lead a mission to his church. 'David Sheppard asked Jim to take this on. Twice a week over a period of six months and after a day's work, Jim, occasionally accompanied by Janet, would meet with local Christians in their homes, together with those from the community who had been specially invited. During our time there, several came to a personal faith in Jesus. Jim also contributed to the scheme set up by the Rev. Ted Roberts in training local men for the ordained ministry in Bethnal Green.'

From the beginning it was felt that Canning Town should be made aware of its own responsibilities to the Centre. It was decided not to use the large chapel initially and to make its refurbishment the responsibility of the local congregation. In the meantime a club room was stripped down and repainted for the Sunday service use. In 1965 the big chapel was opened. Apart from a £350 grant from the diocese the £1,800 needed was raised by the congregation. The job of washing and painting two coats on the interior walls took twenty or so teenagers eight days to complete and a number of the same young people were attending the evening service on Sundays.

In 1967 a milestone was reached with the creation of the local committee. Although local people had been taking a lead in many parts of Mayflower life the decisions about policy had until then been taken by the council and the staff, all drawn from outside the area. The local committee was an elected body of fifteen who would be specially responsible for running and financing the chapel — transport, holidays, Sunday Group work, adult group and the salaries of the chaplain and lady worker. The council would remain trustees in broad terms of the Mayflower 'vision'. They would continue to be responsible for the running and financing of the open youth work, the club buildings, the nursery school and the hostel. They would also continue to appoint all staff after consultation with the local committee.

A 1968 issue of the *Log of the Mayflower* commented. 'After ten years there is much to be thankful for.' But it went on to say:

There are also many questions to be asked. Other Christian groups in industrial areas of the great cities have got so far — a congregation of about a hundred adults who are committed to Christ and His Church. Few such groups seem to have progressed much further. A new religious community has been brought into being. It turns inwards upon itself; its staff give all their time to the pastoral care of Christians; its active members became trapped in so many meetings that they have no time left to meet their neighbours. We face all these problems here. The 64,000 dollar question is 'How can we provide the right stimulus to thought and activity for our Christians to grow up in the faith, and at the same time remain a "Church of the Frontier"?' The danger of enthusiastic activism is that we become so busy giving out that we have no time to take in.

There were very real tensions. Jim and Janet Gosling remember that 'it was a held principle that faith, if it is to grow and develop, needs testing by involvement and commitment. These challenges were supplied to us in no small measure and we found both our single and married life taken up in endless meetings, club and group work, visiting other churches to talk about the work of Mayflower, helping with bazaars, garden fêtes and social events.'

Mary Watts writes.

I was at Mayflower most evenings of the week. My half-day from the shop was spent cleaning the small chapel, my bedroom at home and visiting four old people. Sundays I took morning nursery class (30 or more children, with Jean Kitchener). Sunday afternoons were spent preparing for next week's lesson. Then there was evening church, after church, questions and Bible study. Our visiting list for home evangelism grew and grew. Holidays were with Church camps in which we were helpers and organizers. We never noticed any danger signals and in my mind perhaps, I felt the Lord would return any time. Colin and I had our first child, Sarah, in 1966. It was a difficult birth and it was not a good time for both of us. I was told by the doctor it was a miracle Sarah was born alive! Nonetheless, on returning home I was immediately whizzing around at Mayflower trying to disguise a growing confusion and depression.

Because of so many callers at our front door it was impossible to have times of quiet and privacy. I found myself hiding under my bed as I did when a child when bombs fell during the war.

• • •

Colin adds.

'At the time of our first "break" with Mayflower (or should it be breakdown) we were visiting some 48 families as well as all the other activities. Mary and I had no more to give. Our time was never our own – we only had one front door (unlike staff at Mayflower), no days off, no family time, no sabbaticals!!'

• • •

These tensions were at the heart of much of the debate about the future vision during the next stage of Mayflower's development. But they were the result of real success in reaching the local community with the gospel. Following Jesus was clearly on the agenda in Canning Town.

A Life-Changing Call
David Sheppard

It was one of those walks and talks with God which settle the direction of your life. I had shared the dream I had for the Dockland Settlement buildings in Canning Town with Hugh Gough, the Bishop of Barking. The Dockland Settlement committee was prepared to hand them over to the Bishop of Barking's committee. A new start with new leadership seemed possible; but did I really believe God was calling me to be part of it? I was a curate in Islington, looking forward to marrying Grace in two months' time.

Late at night I drove to Canning Town and walked all round its streets, talking to God and trying to listen to Him. I remember saying, 'Lord, we say we believe You are God the Father Almighty, and that, if we have plenty of trees and gardens, we can bring up children the way You want them brought up. But not here. In this kind of crowded inner-city area, we don't believe that it's possible.' I felt God's honour was at stake: if it is not possible to work this out for inner-city people, then I cannot believe in God. I sensed strongly His calling to me to come and play a part in working out a better plan for the Church in the inner city and for the inner city itself. That midnight

David Sheppard

conversation has remained central to my motivation ever since.

We talked a lot about the Vision during those first years of the Mayflower's life. I always said there were two parts to the vision: first was to establish a strong, locally rooted church. Second was to serve the neighbourhood with the very considerable resources that the Church was given. The two parts fed each other.

A locally rooted church needed to work out its faith in the context of the district where God placed it. That involved taking the trouble to find out the needs of the area and the issues which concerned people. It didn't mean that Christians should always go along with the majority opinion: it did mean refusing to shut our eyes to the tensions, pain and arguments of our neighbours. It meant being there in many parts of local life. As a new company of local Christians grew, so a new caring force was coming into being to serve the neighbourhood.

In turn the youth and community work of the Centre kept the church fellowship from forgetting that the Church exists for the sake of other people: the presence of teenagers who were quite new to the order and stillness of the evening service could be irritating to the congregation — or it could be a reminder of God's calling to us to live and worship so that the world might believe. There was a good moment of meeting of these parts of the vision when Joe prayed in the Sunday Group, 'And thank You, Lord, that Mrs Olley didn't shoo us as much as she used to.'

Always we believed there should be an evangelistic thrust to our work: to start with there were six communicants and twenty present for our biggest Sunday services. Many of the first people who joined our church were finding a haven where their personal hurts could find attention and care — bereaved or lonely, young people in trouble, sick in mind or body. It's honourable when the Church is seen to be the kind of place where hurt people can find a haven. But it's very difficult for a congregation to be outgoing if it is largely made up of those who feel they need protection from the world.

We coined the phrase that the majority of our neighbours were 'happy pagans', and that the gospel of Christ was for them as much as for those who more quickly saw their need. The great majority of people in Canning Town had never been churchgoers, as all the figures show since the rows of terraced houses were hurriedly built around the Victoria and Albert Docks in the 1850s. Many wished us well in what we offered to young people, the poor and the elderly. It was usually a long time before such 'happy pagans' began to feel that this Christ could be for them.

When Roy Trevivian was chaplain at the Mayflower, years after we had moved on, he told me that a man I knew well had committed himself to the Christian journey. He had been away with an adult group from the Mayflower when the penny dropped: he told Roy that he had to see that these Christians really cared about Canning Town, and he had seen this during the weekend. Roy and I traced back more than fifteen years from when Grace and I started to visit that man's home: it included going to football together, long conversations about the children and about the needs of the neighbourhood. As we remembered the unchurched background of so many Canning Town people, we agreed that we should not be surprised that effective evangelism would often take many years of friendship and patient contact. We needed to earn the right to speak of our faith.

Often it was in the middle of the common life we experienced together that deep conversations about life and faith would bubble up. Today I find it hard to hear myself think if I'm in a crowded room with the music turned up to full volume. I used to be able to manage much better: I remember very serious conversations with teenagers standing three or four feet away from the record player in Club House, with a noisy crowd around us. Somehow we were given a pool of stillness for a few minutes; they felt safe to talk in that context, when to be invited to talk alone in a silent room would have scared them into frozen silence.

Weekends away often provided the relaxed moments when long and deep discussions took place. I ran a week's cricket tour in Sussex in two different years. On one of these I was driving the minibus; we passed a Bible text on a small chapel, 'The wages of sin is death, but the gift of God is eternal life.' 'That's not right, Skipper, is it?' said Ted. 'What's not right?' 'Trying to frighten people into being Christians.' A lively discussion followed. Ted felt he had been pressurized when he was much younger in the Covenanter group and had turned his back on Church. The Teenage Club offered him common ground on which as a lively and sometimes disruptive member he kept in contact with the Christian body. Years on he found his way into the Sunday Group; his journey led on to becoming a reader in the local church and later to ordination.

The Oxford-College style of the courtyard built by the Dockland Settlement seemed to me to carry with it an unspoken assumption of the superiority of middle-class culture coming to a working-class community. As the Mayflower team came into being, I felt it instructive to draw the parallel with missionary work in other parts of the world. Suppose we were called to India, I hope we should have learned not to say that we came from Europe, home of superior culture, wisdom and truth; rather that we came from a different culture to a different culture and needed to listen and learn carefully from that different culture. We too needed to respect the distinct culture of Canning Town and not impose behaviour patterns we had learned in another culture.

Looking back, I realize that we sometimes defended Canning Town right or wrong. It wasn't all neighbourly and heart-warming. But perhaps we needed to love uncritically for a while before we arrived at the discernment which could test what was wholesome and what was destructive. I was much more confident that I could do that during the second half of our twelve years in Canning Town. Learning such discernment meant avoiding ready-made packs of rules. During my first years in Canning Town I read Ted Wickham's book *Church and People in an Industrial City*; he said that evangelical Christians were 'moralizers'. I recoiled from the word. I believed the Evangelical Gospel centred on the unreserved love of our Lord Jesus Christ; it was by grace we were saved, not by works. But then, I thought further about evangelical taboos which suggested that you could deal with the spirit of worldliness by a code of Thou shalt not; perhaps Ted Wickham was right. If we were constantly condemning the behaviour of our neighbours, we should never reach the place where they would hear about the love of Christ and the goodness of the Creator, God.

Real morality is what we bind upon ourselves, because we've thought matters out for ourselves. 'Seen my new watch, Mr Burton? asked Jim, flashing his fine wristwatch in front of him. 'Yes, Jim.' 'How much do you think I paid for it?' 'How much?' 'Only five quid.' 'That's very good, isn't it?' George Burton wasn't rising. He knew as much as anyone about goods which fell off the back of lorries. He wanted Jim to think his morality out for himself. It was two or three years later when Jim brandished another watch; 'See my new watch, Mr Burton? How much do you think it cost me?' 'I don't know, Jim. How much did it cost you?' 'Thirty-seven pounds,' he said with heavy emphasis. He had learned for himself a major lesson about honesty.

We realized how bookish the Church often is, and how much that added to the gap which our neighbours sensed between them and church life. We had soon introduced a bookstall at the back of the church, as was expected of well-run churches. Some time later it dawned on us that this was the first impression newcomers received on entering the church; it said loud and clear to many people, 'Being a proper Christian involves reading lots of books.' In most homes in Canning Town books were no part of the scene. I wrote a column in *Woman's Own* throughout our Mayflower years; quite often a man would say to me, 'I saw what you wrote in my wife's book.'

We came to the conclusion that the bookstall shouted a message which added to the sense that the church was part of a foreign culture. We removed it from the chapel and moved it to an inconspicuous place where those who came to Fellowship Hour after the service could find it.

Equally foreign was the rule of life which insisted that all thoughtful Christians must read part of the Bible every day.

It dawned on me that printing was only invented in the fifteenth century; there were many wonderful Christians before that who would not have been able to own their own Bible. So I would say that there were three ways in which people took the Bible into their system, not just one way; when they heard it read and explained in church, when they read and discussed it in a group and when they had a go at reading it for themselves. I hoped that all three ways would be possible for us. People are more likely to build on what they recognize they are doing already than through being made to feel guilty at what they are not doing.

When I wrote about this in the *Log of the Mayflower*, I had letters from graduate Christians, grateful for a sense of release from a code of rules they found they couldn't keep. They had felt so guilty at failing to keep up with reading the Bible every day that they couldn't bring themselves to read it at all.

I learned much in our Mayflower years about being 'members one of another' in Paul's words. My background led me to have an ideal of the individual who stood on his own two feet. Canning Town taught me to think more corporately. When I looked again at the Bible, I realized that we were to bear one another's burdens in the body of Christ. Nothing taught me this so much as Grace's two illnesses — first going through the very dark tunnel of nervous illness and then a major operation for cancer. We learned that God does not promise to protect His children from every painful experience: He does promise to stay close to us through those tunnels. And at so many moments when we might feel deserted, He makes sure that someone is there who can minister His love to us. The acceptance and support of the Mayflower Family through those long times of Grace's illness were major factors in helping us to survive those difficult times, and her to live the very full life she does today.

Discussion in groups — 'Talking groups' — became a regular feature of Mayflower life; Grace and I would meet with other couples in someone's home or in our flat; others came together in the Searching Group, study groups, Fellowship Hour, the Sunday Group. I met one evening with a Searching Group which the chaplain, Brian Seaman, had been leading; I asked them to tell me how it worked for them and made some notes of what they said.

'Nobody made you feel silly.'

'You learned to talk to others.'

'In an argument you let yourself go.'

'It's all part of your training, though you don't know it.'

'You learn to respect other people's point of view.'

'Your mind's working all the time.'

The most crucial hurdle for people to surmount was that of self-confidence; many highly intelligent people put themselves down because their intelligence has been trampled on, whether at home or at school. We were discussing this at the Mayflower when Jack said, 'Yes, the teachers always noticed the bright ones at the front and we illiterates sat at the back and mucked about.' Slowly through the life of the Mayflower he was learning to put away that destructive self-picture, that he was an illiterate. It took courage to recognize that God had in fact given him a very quick mind, and that he should not always shrink away from taking a lead. When we established the local committee, members were very ready to take on responsibility as their confidence grew.

We learned to work 'with the grain'; if we organized a weekend away, it would not have a tidy series of sessions with a logical chain of subjects. The weekend would be time, often quite late in the evening, for discussion. Often that would go on far into the night as people dug deep into human and spiritual issues. An academic surgeon from the London Hospital came to talk to some forty adults about the ethics of transplants. Perhaps three of them had in their schooldays passed the eleven-plus. They pushed him for over two hours' keen questioning. He said afterwards, 'I was as exhausted as I am by my brightest students.'

Getting over the hurdle of self-confidence remains the key to the development of local leadership. Since my Mayflower years I have never doubted that God gives intelligence and ability in every community. Nothing is more important to me in Liverpool Diocese's response to the report 'Faith in the City' than what we call GUML (Group for Urban Ministry and Leadership). In some twenty Urban Priority Area parishes there is a small team going through two years of training or already commissioned. Belonging to the team helps confidence to develop and local leadership grows stronger both within the life of the Church and in serving the wider community.

I learned much myself from these many talking groups. Two women took me on in one discussion: 'Why don't you ask other vicars to preach and teach us? Do you think you've got to protect us?' It made me realize that local Christians could think for themselves; the Holy Spirit teaches through the different insights and experience of other members of the body of Christ. I started to invite other clergy. As I've continued on my journey, I have come to believe that we have a richer understanding, as we open ourselves up to Christians, of other churches and traditions. In Liverpool the bitter sectarian divisions between Protestant and Catholic were a very serious block in the way of the gospel. We don't agree about everything, but we are much richer for listening to one another and for joining hands in serving the world around us.

Our emphasis on local leadership meant that the residents who came to live in the hostel were carefully briefed about their role at the Mayflower; they were not invited to run things but to offer support to a local work which was growing. If a local person emerged with the necessary gifts for a task they had been undertaking, the residents would be asked to step back. We had a noble army of residents; they were enormously willing to tackle menial jobs. They provided loyal undergirding to much of our work. They offered a friendly presence in many activities in which local people came to the Mayflower. I have met former residents playing major parts in the life of the Church and of voluntary and statutory services, often in Urban Priority Areas. Many tell me that the Mayflower opened their eyes to what God was calling them to be and to do.

As I look back on our Mayflower years many of my memories are associated with the old club block, replaced long ago by a more functional building. It was used by many who did not come to the church. The belief which underlay all that caring and effort was that 'The earth is the Lord's and everything in it, the world and all its inhabitants,' and the Lord's promise, 'I have come that they might have life and have it abundantly.' Many people in Canning Town grew up without opportunities to enjoy abundant life. The nursery school and its parents' group, the youth club, the mums and the granddads all offered some opening for good fellowship and for developing confidence and personal gifts.

In the middle of my memories of the youth work stands the large figure of George Burton; David and Jean Hewitt's excellent book about him struck the right note in its title, *A Study in Contradictions*. Thinking of George has often reminded me of the part in Paul about God's treasure being put in earthenware pots. George was very earthy. The burst of temper, the brash boasting, the personal fears remained part of his makeup until his death, though many of these were partially healed. But George knew what it was to be a man accepted in Christ; the pot was earthy, but the treasure was in it. There was an astonishing tenderness, a jump ahead of knowing what others feared, a powerful faith in Christ, when at ease an ability which was quite out of the ordinary to handle the roughest youngsters, taking their hates and bringing about riotous fun, lifting their horizons of what life could be in East London.

There were two tiers to the youth work — open clubs and the Sunday Group. When George Burton died, we could not find a youth leader for quite a while. That gap was so wide that I laid down my other work and became senior youth leader for twelve months, until John Roberts joined us. It was the most demanding job I have ever done. If I had not seen George do it, I would not have dared risk such a free and easy atmosphere. There were separate rooms for judo or weight-training or hairdressing, or the playground for football or cricket. But the Teenage Club centred around the clubhouse, with a canteen in the middle, plenty of noise from the records, snooker tables, table tennis and darts. These activities made a contribution but they weren't the club. The club was people and was built around friendships. Helpers who came regularly made a club evening personal. Grace Spencer, a middle-aged member of the local church, ran the canteen for years; many of our most awkward members had personal and deep conversations with her. One girl wandered back into the club after being away for several months. 'Where's Pam?' was her first question. The feature of the club to which she was looking forward was renewing her friendship with a voluntary helper. Thank God, Pam, who travelled every Monday evening from an office job in the City was indeed there, and the girl was not disappointed.

Joining the Sunday Group included the commitment to coming to church on a Sunday evening. We were very aware of Sunday Group evenings as they met, often noisily, in George Burton's flat which was immediately above ours. They spent a lot of time together every week, with weekends and holidays away. Joining the group seemed to

Viscount Montgomery visits the boxing club – 1959

set its members free to think about life and about God; it was as though together they took one step towards Christ. A good number moved on, one by one to faith in Christ. Pat said, 'We used to have quite a few discussions and arguments and films. I just couldn't believe in it. Well, I don't think I really wanted to . . . They had something I hadn't got. I felt that I wanted this thing, but I was slow, dozy, couldn't be bothered.' Later she realized that she did 'want this thing'. Len, who later married her, also took a long time to think seriously about Christianity; 'I didn't like talking about it, because I didn't want to be involved.' After a year or more in the group he said that he prayed, 'Jesus Christ, I believe in you. Will you accept me?'

It's twenty-four years since Grace and I moved from Canning Town. I look back on the twelve years we spent at the Mayflower with great thankfulness as the biggest education of my life. I see my journey since then as following a very straight line. I want to encourage the Church to grow in two directions: to be outward-looking, ragged-at-the-edges, involved in the messy and hurting human experience which our neighbours face, with plenty of stepping stones on which we may meet them. And at the same time to be a Church in which there is deep commitment to Jesus Christ, with our spiritual roots being refreshed both personally and in the fellowship of the body of Christ and as we serve him in a hurt world.

Twelve Fulfilling Years
Grace Sheppard

I was in a bit of a whirl when we arrived at Mayflower.

David and I had married in June 1957. During our engagement we had discussed the Bishop of Barking's invitation to David to become the next warden. David had accepted, so we knew that after just a few months in Islington, where he was curate, we would be moving again. He was asked to make a new beginning as this Dockland Settlement was struggling to survive. We were both in our twenties and ready for anything.

But this enthusiasm was to receive a rude interruption. During our honeymoon in Italy I suffered a bad attack of chickenpox and was admitted to hospital where I stayed for ten days in isolation. When the spots subsided I returned to Islington where, with no time for convalescence, we set up home together in the curate's lodgings in July. On 1st August, David became warden of the newly named Dockland Family Centre, spending two days a week in Canning Town. He was exhilarated with the possibilities of the new work.

But I was struggling with a frightening lack of self-confidence, exhausted by the excitement of the wedding, the move and the effects of the virus. In September I broke down in Holborn Underground station, fighting for breath.

I was receiving psychotherapy in a London clinic when we moved once more in January 1958. I came on the day to watch our bits of furniture loaded onto the van bound for London's Dockland. It was our second home in six months. I felt frustrated and inadequate.

Still shell-shocked from the events of the previous months, I finally left the clinic and began to make a new life in the married quarters carved out for us from a hostel corridor on the first floor in the Cooper Street building. We put in a front door with a knocker and painted it primrose yellow. This was to let us be private when we wished. Earlier we had been to visit Sir Reginald Cox who had lived there many years before. He said, referring to the little room on the back staircase, 'You could get a little maid.' That room was later used to house the communal washing machine. Needless to say I never had a little maid.

It was the electrician who called during my first fortnight who brought me to myself. The floorboards were up in the kitchen where he was working. There were wire guards on our windows which looked out onto waste ground and a scrapyard where fierce Alsation dogs walked up and down.

'Do you think you're going to like it here?' he said. His directness shook me. My heart sank as I was not sure that I would like it and did not want to tell him so and risk upsetting him or giving the impression of being standoffish.

'Oh, yes,' I said. 'People have been very kind.'

'You hesitated then,' he said.

Feeling vulnerable, I acknowledged that in time I thought that I would settle, but that it was a bit difficult at first. That felt better and I stopped patronizing him with protective half-truths and became more sincere and open. We talked more freely. That encounter set the tone for me. I realized

I could not hide my problems from local people and that they had a right to know what I was feeling now that I was on their territory. It was an important step on my road to wholeness.

There had been no briefing on the lifestyle and culture of Canning Town people. We simply came as we were, young, inexperienced, eager and newly married. We were getting used to each other at the same time as getting to know the many people who became our friends over the next twelve years. I had been sent to serve stripped of my self-confidence. As it happened, this gave us both an insight we needed and might never have had otherwise. For instance, I had become terrified of attending church, feeling trapped by the formality. We were to meet dozens of people of ability who lacked confidence for other reasons. There was the man who told me he had to drink a stiff whisky before going to church, and the woman who stood outside in her bedroom slippers saying she was not good enough to come in. She had been looking at those who came for weeks and felt they were all confident, smart people unlike herself. I knew a little of what they felt. I knew the last thing they needed was a push. They needed, in George Burton's immortal words, 'time, love and understanding' until they were ready.

One day we decided to ask a few people round for a meal in our flat. We had furnished one of the rooms as a formal dining room with wedding presents — an antique mahogany dining table and six chairs. We invited a small number of guests including people from Canning Town as well as elsewhere. My brother joined us from the City. As our guests arrived, I began to panic. In our new posh dining room, something felt out of place. It felt too formal. I didn't feel myself, and I wanted everyone to feel relaxed. Suddenly I disappeared to get a tablecloth to cover the shiny mahogany. I produced a pot of tea and put it on a mat in the middle of the table, also a radio which I turned on to provide soft background music. The atmosphere changed and we all began to relax.

We sold the table and chairs soon afterwards. We were allowed to knock down a wall between the kitchen and the dining room making a larger more informal living space. We bought more appropriate furniture. Here we entertained both local people and visitors like the Bishop of Southwark, Edward Boyle and Sir Donald Allen equally comfortably.

During those first years we combined finding our feet as a married couple in a different culture with new responsibilities and with the challenge of living in a community made up of staff and residents.

But it was the arrival of George Burton that influenced me most. He frightened me at first. His openness contrasted with my initial lack of confidence. Yet his forthright manner, his uncompromising Christianity and his clear sense of God's calling ran alongside a deep sensitivity and love of children. They trusted him. We have a photograph of George sitting on the floor in our daughter Jenny's room. He is sitting in a circle having tea with her and her dolls and teddies. He drank a real cup of tea. Jenny still remembers this. His ability to give his full attention to one little girl was not unusual. He loved and respected children for he never lost touch with the child in himself.

Having had a traumatic adolescence himself, he also understood the needs and aspirations of young people. They trusted him too. He was gentle with hurt people and rough with insincere people. I felt he understood me though he was a little cautious with me at times, perhaps because I was the boss's wife even though I was young. He had, however, little experience of working in a team. This was a trial to him at times and he was inclined to lay down the law. But we all grew up and learnt to stand up to him sometimes while realizing at other times that he was as vulnerable as the rest of us. That he was prepared to disclose his own fears from time to time made the rest of us face our own more readily. We were all convinced he was the right man for the job, so that when he threatened to leave we met to pray that he would stay.

As well as such an ignominious start, two other events put extra strain on our little family. In 1965 when Jenny was three, I was admitted to hospital with cancer. It was difficult to know at first whether to tell the church straightaway or not. Our emotions were in turmoil and yet we knew that if we did it would release a flood of loving care and prayer. After a fortnight we let it be known. Jack Wallace, the chairman then, visited me in hospital. Anxious I suppose not to appear to be malingering, I told him how being laid aside like this enabled me to pray for everyone back home. He was very angry with me. He said, 'Your job is to concentrate on getting better. You can leave the rest to us.' I collapsed into tears of relief and began to relax.

I had many visitors, but towards the end of my treatment, someone came whom I was not expecting. The door to my room opened and in came a small woman wearing a headscarf. She was carrying a bunch of flowers. She dropped the flowers on my bed and said, ''Eer 'are pet lamb.' Then she was gone before I could even say thank you. Mrs Evett had come very occasionally to events at the Mayflower. That day she had caught a bus from Canning Town to Whitechapel. She herself was suffering from cancer from which she soon died. That kind of costly love stays with you. There was a lot of that at the Mayflower.

A second event took place after a day at Southend in the notorious coach. I had been out with a group from the Mayflower and as usual the coach had broken down, so we did not return home until 1.30 a.m. Arriving in our flat, I found David still up. He looked ashen. He asked me to sit down while he made a cup of tea. Then he told me that the

Bishop of Southwark had invited him to consider being the next Bishop of Woolwich, following John Robinson. I was stunned. Recovering quickly, I jumped up and flung my arms round his neck. Whatever his decision, it was a sign that his work was appreciated, that he had not 'buried himself' in Docklands as some had suggested. In fact he had been trained without knowing it. For myself, I was ambitious enough to feel relieved that my breakdown early on had apparently not been a handicap to such an invitation. Also I secretly felt that David was becoming tired and had given all he had. He needed a new challenge.

After the shock came disbelief. But we had agreed with the Mayflower church that after twelve years we were to take a sabbatical. We had a terraced house lined up in Edinburgh and a school place for Jenny. Then came the doubts. I could not see myself as a bishop's wife. We were both still in our thirties. Fantasies about the formality, the expectations and the relative isolation terrified me. We had to test the call. What kind of guidance was this? How could we tell the church? 'They'll never come back,' some had said when we had told them about the sabbatical.

In the church fellowship a tradition of openness had been built up over the years. It was important that if David were to accept the invitation, he would want to go with their blessing. He would want them to know before it became public. He was a well-known figure and the announcement would attract a wide press. We had been sworn to secrecy by Bishop Mervyn. Nothing must leak. To tell more than one or two felt dangerous. Trusting more would be madness. They would have to keep the confidence.

In the end, with Bishop Mervyn's permission, we entrusted the news to all sixteen members of the local committee. They came up to our flat and David made the announcement. Grace Spencer broke the tense silence, 'Oh, well,' she said, 'He got there on our backs, didn't he!' After

War damage was around for a long time

that we talked and prayed. We were clear from then on that we had the support of the church representatives. Not a word leaked out. On 28th February 1969 it was announced and we prepared to leave Canning Town after twelve fulfilling years.

Young People First
(1958-1969)

FOR MOST OF its hundred years of life on this site, work with young people has been the dominant activity. There has been the feeling that adults have already established ways of thinking and behaving and if you can influence young people you can have a much bigger impact on the community. When Mayflower began in 1958 the concentration on youth work was greatest because:-

a) Dockland Settlement had a big club at work with a range of rooms to resource it.

b) David Sheppard had a particular interest in developing a new form of youth work which would reach unchurched families in inner-city areas and provide a training ground for youth leaders.

c) George Burton arrived soon after the reopening of clubs and his personality and concern for young people became a dominant force.

George himself was quite clear about the direction. Acknowledging that Mayflower's activities ranged from a nursery school to the Grandfather's Club he wrote:

We have not felt it right to concentrate on the old and infirm. Rather we see the reaching of teenagers as a priority, for teenagers are the men and women of the future. Ours is a long-term vision, since

Mayflower's first staff team: George Burton, Jean Lodge Patch, Dilys Gething, Joan de Torre, Margaret Fish, Hilary Harman, Grace and David Sheppard

leaders cannot be produced overnight and it is with this fact in mind that we see our work among teenagers as the spearhead of our activity.[1]

...

From the beginning there was also a consciousness of the type of teenager to attract and the tension involved.

It is not easy to run a club for both the law-breaking type and the law-abiding type at the same time. I would rather win for the Lord two of those who do not conform than twenty of the other type because of the impact the former would have on their mates. Furthermore, the majority of clubs are run for the 'better type' – they are well catered for. People talk about 'unclubbable' youngsters, meaning the sort who are too rough to fit into a youth club. I admit that not every boy or girl has the inclination to join a club and in this sense can be called unclubbable, but the term is more often a club leader's excuse for taking the easy way out. There is no boy whom the love of Christ cannot win. The word unclubbable seems to me to be an admission of defeat. [2]

George set out a typical club evening in the early '60s. It remained more or less the pattern until the mid-'80s.

The door is opened at eight o'clock with games equipment laid out in advance and voluntary helpers positioned at strategic points throughout the club. The record player is blaring as the members come in, and this continues at something approaching maximum volume for the whole evening, for they feel most at ease when there is plenty of noise in the background. Usually a helper is at the door to collect subs as they come in, and while he will do his best to squeeze some money out of them he is unlikely to make an issue with someone who refuses point-blank to pay. I should not like to have to face Christ in the Judgment and hear that I deprived any boy or girl of hearing the way of salvation because they had not paid their subs.

The main centre of attraction is the canteen brightly lit at the far end of the club room. A brisk trade is carried on in sweets and soft drinks, and this is frequently combined with some profitable conversation between members and the helpers serving them. The girls usually congregate at one end of the canteen around the record player, and they also have a room of their own upstairs.

The boys play table tennis and snooker in the main club and football in a room upstairs. We have a boxing gym which I let the boys use from time to time, but we have not yet had a professional instructor to coach them. Weightlifting was a popular activity for some time, but it has now dropped out of the picture. All the activities we run are judged according to whether they help or hinder the Christian purpose of the club.

The end of the evening is an important time, for it is the last few minutes of a club night that they mainly remember. We expect very high spirits in the last ten minutes when many of them try to pack into that time all the fun they can, and it is generally during this period that the snooker balls start to fly off the tables. The canteen closes at five to ten, and at ten o'clock I start clearing the club beginning from the canteen end (farthest from the door).[3]

The pattern was also set for communicating the good news of Jesus Christ. George did not believe that it was enough to say that there were Christian helpers and a Christian atmosphere in the club. Young people couldn't guess the gospel truths from the atmosphere of a Christian club.

I thought it right to have a short talk once a week, sometimes concluding with a prayer. I have found it best to hold the service in the middle of the evening as this gives time for latecomers to arrive, and does not dampen down the high spirits which I expect and even encourage at the end of the club evening. Now that the pattern has been established they listen quietly and tolerantly for about twelve minutes, but after that they become restless and soon let you know that they have had enough.

Outside speakers are not encouraged, for we have found that a speaker known to the members in the club received a better hearing.[4]

...

The question of the individual or the group was a delicate one. George wrote:

I usually believe in keeping a natural group together, because when one or two are converted I want them to be able to influence the others, and they cannot do this if they have cut themselves off from their circle of friends. But if you want to talk to one or two about Christ it is not easy while their mates are there. You will not get their confidence. They will not tell you the story that they lie on their bed sometimes and say a little prayer. Keep their confidence, that's important.

Since it is this personal relationship between the leader and individual club members that is the essence of Christian club work, we should not be too concerned about numbers. In some cases excessive numbers can be a positive disadvantage, especially if you have not got many helpers in your club. [5]

This is where the resident system was of so much advantage. Rosemary Finch remembers. 'We had a large team here. George was very much person-centred. He would go out of his way to help an individual. He could do that because he didn't actually have to run the club. He had people that were doing that while he could spend the evening sitting, just talking to one individual. You couldn't do that in a normal youth club because the staff ratio is so small that you need to be around. He never let go — if he felt God had given him somebody by name he stuck at that person. It was tenacity and perseverance.'

From the beginning, running clubs took their toll. George Burton again:

There is the bad language, the dirty jokes, the indifference to the gospel message. Then there is the damage to your property, to your dignity and perhaps to your person. Windows will go, doors will be smashed, equipment will be broken. Sometimes the damage will be unintentional or the result of high spirits. Sometimes it will be deliberate and malicious as on the evening when Jean and I found the upstairs part of the club in a terrible state: Mansion Polish smeared on the ceiling and walls, sand thrown all over the corridors, doors and windows broken. We closed the club and prayed together, and then I went out in my car and met the same boys a few streets away and started to talk to them. I did not scold them but had a laugh with them, and then quite casually said, 'Well, I must go back and give Miss Lodge Patch a hand to clean up.' They all wanted to come back and help, but I picked out four or five of the ringleaders and took them back in the car, and they worked very hard clearing up the mess. Incidentally, we learned that night not to leave such tempting missiles around![6]

· · ·

There were limitations to the effectiveness of open club work in terms of Christian conversions. George wrote: '. . . the spearhead of our teenage work at the Mayflower has been what we call the "groups". While our clubs are open for all to join, admission to the groups is by invitation only. It is here that we have seen the most obvious fruit of our activity over the past few years.'[7]

Over a period George brought together a group of young people called the Sunday Group who went up to George's flat most nights of the week. They played records, drank endless cups of tea and talked. It was a place to go away from home — a place where they felt free. The flat soon became a shambles. There was litter everywhere. Furniture was broken. But this was their natural way of behaving and George accepted it.

No alcohol and no kissing or even holding hands were about the only rules. On Sundays they used to come up to the flat just after two o'clock and stay together right through to ten o'clock. Often they went out together for the afternoon in the minibus, up to London or out to Epping Forest or further afield. Going to church together made it a lot easier for them. They also went away for weekends and even holidays abroad. There were rows, jealousies and disagreements but these were talked through as far as possible. George made a point of visiting the parents to give them confidence in what their children were doing and he kept the numbers to about twelve.

There were no set Bible studies or formal talks. Discussion or 'argument' as the members called it was the

Rather you than me – early Girls Club Work Party

main feature covering almost everything — homes, schools, colour bar, marriage and love. George did more listening than talking but would feed in Christian things — something to make them think. He would always visit if one of the members failed to turn up and over a period built up a very powerful relationship with each person. He was happy to sit up late at night with an individual after the rest of the group went home.

George and Jean began to see fruit from their labour. There was no sudden flood of conversions, but gradually and individually these young people came to Christ. They included Ted Lyons, Jim and Janet Gosling, Pat and Len Howells, Bill and Doreen Turner and Alan and Rita Dennis — all single at the time of their conversion but getting married later on.

Initially they not only came to Christ in the Sunday Group but grew as Christians there. There was no insistence on a daily Bible reading though a weekly Bible study led by one of the Sunday Group leaders developed. They were encouraged to attend the church's confirmation classes led by David Sheppard. George wrote: 'Our aim is that these young converts should go on to become mature Christians with a deep faith in Christ and an ability to relate their faith to their everyday lives and problems. We believe that if the foundations are to be solid this may take a long time. We don't want to produce "spiritual mushrooms". We pray that ultimately each one will become an active member of our local church and find a useful sphere of service within it.'[8]

Part of the growth was an encouragement into service and members of the group visited people in hospital, ran social evenings for their parents and relatives, helped at Mayflower functions, decorated needy families' houses and even prepared for and ran their own camp.

They were also fed back into the clubs as leaders and often ran their own groups. Rosemary Finch remembers. 'One of the keys of the Sunday Group was to plough people back into leadership, so you had groups like the 69 Group. You had Jim and Janet's group, you had Pat and Len's group. You had a number of the Tuesday night groups. They were part of the ideal of the local leaders producing more leaders.'

The close way that George worked with the Sunday Group had its risks. Colin Watts who was only a little older than the members of the group and part of the 'adult' church described it as '. . . an élitist band of young local people cosseted along a path to Christian conversion, hand-reared by George and untainted by the church.'

There were bound to be jealousies. Colin and Mary described the way they were sharply criticized on their wedding day for not inviting George with whom they felt they had little contact. Another problem was arrogance. Rita Dennis said, 'I think one of the most arrogant things I ever admit to and feel ashamed of is being a Christian at the Mayflower and the fact that we thought we knew it all. We were the only people in the world that had the right answer. Everybody else had the wrong answer. I think it had been reinforced subtly. Everything was so exciting and breaking new ground. All these people coming from all over the place to look at the Mayflower — and there you were pushed up to the front — these are our young people. We were so cocooned that I think you become arrogant, don't you? You think you're the only way.'

The part prayer played in all this cannot be overestimated. George talks about '. . . constant, earnest, specific prayer for individuals which has formed the common background to all these activities. As the Sunday Group has been developed we have had much to thank God for in the way of specific answers to our prayers. It is indeed true that God "is able to do exceeding abundantly, above all that we ask or think".'[9]

Rosemary Finch remembers: George certainly was a man of prayer. He spent hours going over the names and praying for people. Certainly for two or three years after David Hewitt left I was almost George's batman as it were. I used to go up every morning and take him his breakfast. He would give me various jobs to do during the day. But we'd always spend time actually praying about individuals.'

••••

Mark Birchall remembers an incident in club.

GM was an older lad, sometimes violent, sometimes very helpful in checking violence. One night in 1961 he came in wanting to "have it out" with George and Skipper and really have a fight with them. On several recent evenings he had been high with drink or drugs. This time he was very high. They had half-an-hour in the office while David Hewitt and I lurked outside in case of trouble (not sure what we would have done). GM alternated between raving like a lunatic and arguing noisily – much prayer went up and there was no explosion. He stalked out, and then twenty minutes later came back and apologized to George for everything, which was quite fantastic. George was much moved at the power and protection of God (he was not at all well at the time). At the end of the evening George spoke powerfully to the helpers for five minutes when he had just intended to say good night and thanks.'

...

The youth work being pioneered by Mayflower had a wider significance. Michael Eastman writes. 'The Mayflower has been one of the crucibles in which has been forged new approaches to Christian youth work amongst young people shoved down and pushed out by our society. The great majority are beyond the reach and off the map of most churches.'

George Burton's book, *People Matter More Than Things*, became a classic and influenced many others working in the same field. It was all the more remarkable for being written by someone who was illiterate well into middle life.

A Fellowship of Christian Youth Club Workers had been set up in the mid-1950s. A newsletter was produced and key leaders in the London-based units met regularly. The new Mayflower became part of this network along with Cambridge University Mission, All Souls Clubhouse, Knights Association of Christian Youth Clubs, the Greenhouse and Elizabeth Whitelaw Reid Club. At the same time the Oxford Kilburn Club set up a development committee which sought to promote open youth clubs. David Sheppard served on this committee. Know-how was shared, more of failure than success, mutual self-help and support developed, some practical resources drawn together and the beginnings made of a literature on the practice, theory and theology of such forms of Christian youth ministry.

Before long the work of the Conference, the Fellowship

and the Oxford Kilburn Club Development Committee grew beyond the scope of any one of the units involved, so in 1964 The Frontier Youth Trust for Christian Club Work was set up with its own board of trustees, chaired by John Stott. The work of the new Trust was undertaken by an executive committee, the first secretary of which was David Sheppard. The Mayflower was FYT's first office base with Hilary Harman as administrator. Michael Eastman who was FYT's first staff member and is still the secretary and development officer writes.

People learnt as they did, often painfully, but the experience has been lifelong. Those who today hail 'relational youth work' as the great new discovery of our age need to relearn from that period thirty years ago. Relationship-building is the heart of Frontier Youth work and always has been. So too is learning by doing, not in the abstract but in the particular. Action and reflection in community is the way such learning is developed. Theology is living and dynamic as those engaged in the struggles seek to understand God's mind in Scripture, express God's heart in practice and learn to worship in the midst of joy, pain, frustration, fallibilities, horrors and hopes of the everyday life of raw and flawed adults in the making on the underside of a great city.

One further initiative which had wider implications was the series of booklets, *Arguing, Loving, Belonging* and *Working* published by Scripture Union. The Sunday Group helped write the books. Michael Eastman again.

These were trail-making booklets and a team effort included Ted Lyons's excellent strip-cartoon versions of the parables brought up to date in East London.

The *Today Series* of Bible Study material, also published by Scripture Union came from that era. These showed it was possible by using contemporary tabloid format to produce printed material with which those in a non-book culture are at home. These are approaches being painfully relearned today. The principles are at the heart of FYT's current national project in this respect . . .

The story of the Sunday Group from those pioneering days has gone into legend. The bunch of energetic, anarchic, creative, vulnerable young people, some labelled 'failures' by the schools and always 'in trouble' who learnt with George, Jean, David and Grace what it meant to become disciples of Jesus the radical, friend of outcasts and sinners, continue to make a difference in the world. Ted Lyons and Jim Gosling are Anglican ministers, Jim being also a probation officer. Alan Dennis was an excellent youth worker, with Rita, his wife. Bill Turner trained at the YMCA College and returned later as the full-time youth worker at the Mayflower.

...

A Canning Town Christian
Ted Lyons's Story

George Burton and David Hewitt blocked my path on the Barking Road. They were out and about rounding up teenagers for their youth club. They invited my mate and myself to meet them at the club. It was called the Mayflower which sounded a cissy name for the area. This robust man with a Scots accent and the younger, posh, slim man with spectacles were certainly not from Canning Town, but they seemed friendly enough for us to go along. The Mayflower premises were not new to me. I had previously been a member of the Dockland Settlement.

I was not fifteen and during the next two or three years there were many occasions when George regretted he had invited me to his club. He didn't just get me but my gang of ten or twelve other boys. We used and abused the club premises and sometimes drove George to despair. On one occasion we turned off all the lights in the five-a-side football hall and hurled iron bars around in the pitch dark. It was a dare. If you were hit that was too bad. Another time darts were hurled around the club room. You had to move fast or be pinned to the wall. We were sometimes banned but always George would let us back in, hoping that we might listen to the gospel. On Wednesday night at the end of club there would be the epilogue. We would often distract others or try and dodge the epilogue altogether. I remember banging on the windows from outside with a billiard cue while George gave an epilogue. We smashed the window and hurled abuse at him. He was furious. He came charging out like a mad bull. We ran for our lives. 'You're chicken, Ted Lyons, ya chicken!' I was chicken. When George was on the warpath most people were chicken! Once again I was banned from the club.

But the Mayflower kept having us back. By then many of us had a love-hate relationship with George and with the out-of-place, middle-class people who helped in the club. They agonized over us, were patient and went on forgiving and talked about Jesus. Often we were unimpressed. However, George was gradually winning my friendship.

'Are you a Christian?' I asked an old school mate as we stood just inside the entrance to the club. 'Yes, I am,' he replied. I was dumbfounded. Bernie had been the captain of the football and cricket teams at my junior school. He was a Canning Town kid and I'd known him since I was five. And he was a Christian! Local teenagers were becoming Christians! This was more threatening than any epilogue.

I was about seventeen and had started playing football for a team in Romford. This loosened my links with the gang and the club. George didn't waste time in seizing the opportunity to visit me at home and invite me to the Sunday Group who had special access to his flat during the week as well as Sunday. I was nervous about going. I didn't want my mates to know I was mixing with Christians. Even as their leader I knew I would be ridiculed and ostracized. All my life I had been in a gang. Strong group identity was the very fibre of my life. Toughness was the order of the day. Now I was being invited into completely foreign territory. I knew I would be letting my mates down. They would think I was going soft. The crunch came when I was walking along alone. Two of my mates were walking towards me. As they approached I heard John say to Jeff that he would bash him if he spoke to me. They walked past in silence. It confirmed my worst fears – I was out on a limb.

I continued with the football and going to the Sunday Group. There was some compensation. Jim was a Christian. He was a big lad, an expert at judo and I knew he had stood up to a tough gang leader in the club. Len had a flat nose and was a real cockney – he was a Christian too. At least I could identify with them and others in the group. They were not as weird as I thought. Over the next several months I expressed my doubts and disbelief in the gospel. But I was outnumbered. Not only George and his team of helpers but a group of Canning Town teenagers spoke about their faith in Jesus and showed it in their lives. Besides it was good to play football and cricket with Bernie again!

An old musket in the corner of George's flat caught my eye. It was old and rusty. For some reason it was part of the furniture before George arrived. He noticed my interest and invited me to clean it for him and also do some research about its history. I eagerly agreed but didn't know what I was letting myself in for. The days of my conversion were now numbered! As I cleaned the rifle in George's flat he would talk to me about Christ. I resented it but was hooked enough on the musket to be drawn into discussion. By now I was just eighteen. The witness of those around me convinced me that Jesus had lived and was still alive, but I had not committed my life to him. For a few months I had been reluctant to take that final step, fighting off the challenge to do so. Rumour would get round that I had become a Christian. My reputation was at stake. Committing myself to Jesus was a great risk. Thank God I took the risk.

One evening I arrived home from work to find my mother looking very sad. She was sitting with my father in the kitchen. She told me that earlier that day my grandfather, 'Pa', had died. I had felt quite close to Pa. He had made a fuss of me and had often taken me out in his lorry when I was a boy. As we drove along he would let me hold the steering wheel while he lit up. I felt sad but God seemed to use my grandfather's death to challenge me. Jesus offered eternal life. I was confronted with the stark reality of death. Would I choose Jesus and life? My parents were unaware of the wrestle that was going on inside. I went upstairs to my bedroom sat on the bed and asked Jesus to come into my life. Jesus had got through. I felt a sense of peace even though I had lost the battle. I had been painting a picture of Christ on the Cross in my bedroom for George. I stood up, looked at the picture and said, 'Before I believed about you, but now I know you.'

I arrived early that night at the club. George was in the clubhouse showing some visitors around. Sister Gemmel of the Church Army had brought a group of women with her from the West End of London. Some of them were alcoholics, others possibly prostitutes. In front of them all, across the room George burst out, 'Ted, are you a Christian?' expecting me to say no. 'Yes,' I said. 'When?' George asked. 'Tonight,' I replied. George nearly fell through the floor. From the look of amazement on his face you would not have known he had been praying for my conversion for some three years. There and then, George said, 'Let's pray to the Lord,' and he thanked God for my conversion. That was in September 1962.

But that was just the beginning. The next few months was a time of enjoying the friendship of the risen Son of God. What a privilege it was to know this very great person, Jesus, and he was my friend. And I was going to live for ever, Great! But the Enemy hadn't finished with me yet. He wasn't going to give me up without a fight. Within six months I was struggling as a Christian. My mother became a Christian shortly after I did and was worshipping regularly at the Mayflower. My dad was confused. He had lost his son to Christianity, now he was losing his wife, and he resented George. I was feeling pressure from members of my family, my workmates and I was seeing some members of the old gang. After six months of my conversion I had stopped going to the Mayflower. The pull of Canning Town was too much for me. My old mates gradually accepted me back and they themselves had given up going to the club. For a good year I

Ted Lyons now

gave up on Christianity. A number of us joined the local boxing club and it was like the old times. George and the Mayflower team must have been deeply saddened by it all.

But the Lord did not give up on me. I remember on one occasion when West Ham won the FA Cup in 1964. During the celebration that went on late into the night, I was holding on to the side of a slow-moving bus at the Boleyn when a beer bottle was dropped from the top of the bus. It hit me on the head and gave me a nasty cut. It stopped me in my tracks and I had to leave for home. If one day I'm bald I will no doubt see the scar! It was as if I'd received a message literally from heaven. 'Ted, you're on the wrong route.'

George had not given up on me either and would occasionally visit my home. My mother kept going to church during this time. Before I drifted away I had started a large painting of the risen Lord appearing to his disciples. It was meant to be another gift to George.

I had the desire to finish it and so I gradually came back to the Mayflower. By then the gang of lads had dwindled. Some were courting and others had grown a bit more mature. One of the gang – the one who threatened to bash the other one if he spoke to me actually started to come to the Mayflower and to church.

George quickly gave me responsibility for a group of thirteen to fourteen-year-old boys. This proved to be a real test for my ability to lead. They were a real handful and on one occasion I was threatened with a knife. George also invited me to run a boxing club and speak sometimes at the epilogue in the main club. By now I was just a bit older than the majority of the members and this helped. Sometimes he would ask me to do unreasonable things and get cross if they were not carried out to his satisfaction. I put up with it because I knew he was testing my loyalty to him. Very sadly within two years of my returning to the Mayflower, George died. Naturally I owe him an enormous debt – in a real sense, my life. But I am indebted to David and Grace Sheppard, to David Hewitt and Jean Lodge-Patch (as she was then called) and to all the residents who enabled George and helped him to love teenagers like me in the 1960s. In many ways George was like a Canning Town kid. He was loud, earthy, totally honest in expressing his feelings, aggressive yet acutely sensitive and vulnerable. Above all, he longed to be accepted and loved. He had a great capacity to love others, especially teenagers with whom he so easily identified.

Along with other members of the Sunday Group my training continued under David Sheppard who started Jim Gosling and myself on the Lay Readers' course. We were raw and unlikely candidates, but were accepted and eventually licensed. During our lay readers' training David Sheppard arranged for Jim and myself to spend one month full time at the London College of Divinity at Northwood (now St John's Nottingham). It was a memorable time for us and them! A year after my licensing at the age of twenty-seven I left the East End for Theological College in Nottingham and was ordained in 1975.

I look back at those early Mayflower days with deep gratitude. I

have become aware of how difficult it was for the Mayflower staff
and residents to work with George. Many of the old Sunday Group
are aware of the great cost to those who worked closely with him.
Thank God that His grace prevailed allowing George to do a mighty
work in the lives of many people, not least my own.

It would appear that then and now accepting Christ is one thing,
continuing with him is another. This is true everywhere but it's
especially true in places like Canning Town where there are powerful
inbred assumptions and expectations. Over the years the East End
has changed but the macho image among young men is as binding
as it was years ago. Those who keep going as Christians have
discovered among other things the macho Jesus who reveals great
courage and true nerve. He accepted the rap, didn't grass on his
mates, took the sentence and died in their place. The certainty is that
this powerful contemporary message for Canning Town will
continue to break the hardest shells and free people to change into
what God wants them to be.

Mayflower holiday in Blankenburg – 1960s

5

The Developing Vision

(1970–1981)

WITH DAVID SHEPPARD'S departure to become Bishop of Woolwich, Denis Downham arrived to be warden. Brian Seaman writes:

I don't think Denis and Edna found life at Mayflower very easy. Skipper had been a very good team manager, building us together, holding us together, leading us forward together. It is never easy to inherit someone else's team, and the large, lively, sometimes argumentative team didn't make it any easier I don't suppose. He was such a gentle, caring man. I sometimes felt that coming to the Mayflower at that stage in its history was biting off more than he could chew. A year after his arrival he was writing in the Mayflower *Log* about low spiritual morale (spring 1971), and he obviously felt this himself.

...

Another contributing factor was finance. There was a considerable drop in donations when David Sheppard left and that was especially hurtful for Denis who had not got David's public profile. By spring 1971 a desperate SOS was printed in the Mayflower *Log* to appeal for more money. Donations were down by 50 per cent, expenditure had been reduced wherever possible, a deficit of over £6,000 was incurred for the year financed by an increased overdraft. Jack Wallace was writing. 'The Mayflower was no longer new. Money which was once gladly given to Canning Town was now needed for similar projects elsewhere. Other East End Christians were looking at Mayflower and wondering whether the large staff and plant were still necessary and whether it was good stewardship to depend to such a large extent on outside resources.

The contradictions were building up. Denis Downham had reiterated Roland Allen's principles for the development of an indigenous church. It was to be self-propagating, self-financing and self-governing. The very creation of the separate Mayflower committee highlighted the problem. The external Mayflower Council continued with responsibility for the wider work. As Brian Seaman writes:

The administration involved in maintaining this latter part of the work was clearly huge, needing the skill, gifts and experience of Christians from wider afield. This made it very difficult to envisage a truly indigenous church. If the Mayflower had been just an ordinary church, with a church building and perhaps a few halls it would have been much easier to envisage the local church taking over complete responsibility for the work. The annual budget for 1972 was £33,878. Could a church of Canning Town people ever meet this? Could there ever be a time when we could manage without the Mayflower Council? Could the warden of such an establishment ever be a local person? Should the wider aspects of the work be phased out so that we could concentrate on building a local church? Was it time to dispense with hostel residents? Should the scaffolding be removed?

• • •

From a local point of view, in addition to the problem of burnout, there were sometimes strained relations with the paid staff and residents. Jim and Janet Gosling comment. 'Not all "paid" members of staff have been "sympathetic" towards those who originally brought into being the vision and likewise did not always see eye to eye with those of us who might have been seen as "enthusiastic amateurs". Such attitudes brought about in many local people, deep and lasting resentment together with feelings of inadequacy. We, like others, have suffered from being the products of others' ambitions and unrealistic expectations, which has caused us a great deal of anxiety and frustration. As a consequence Mayflower has, over the years, lost many valuable and gifted people. Not all, thankfully, have left the Christian faith and some have gone on to achieve much in their spiritual lives.'

On the other hand John Bourne, looking at it from a residents' viewpoint, says: 'It was made clear to us that the residency was a temporary arrangement until the local church took full control of the centre. We were there to be used and carry out duties as and when required. The local people had been told from the Mayflower's earliest days that the Church of England was too middle class and that it was East London culture that was important in developing the work. Baiting residents was a popular sport of some but by no means all locals. This in some introverted way helped raise the confidence of the local church.'

The difficulty was that some local people were already stretched to the limit, but the church still relied heavily on residents and was in danger of exploiting them. If it was to grow to full maturity, it had to take full responsibility for its own activities. In the end if it wanted a weekend away, a social event, a Christmas bazaar, a crèche during Sunday services, baby sitters, the telephone answering, then the members had to provide these for themselves.

There were, however, continuing advances towards the vision of an indigenous church. The Mayflower *Log* was a newssheet produced by the staff every quarter to keep supporters up to date with what was going on at Mayflower. Just before Denis Downham arrived, the first edition of the *Porthole* appeared, very much the product of the local church in the person of Rich Gerard. It had all the wit and humour so characteristic of the East End at that time, and was itself a sign of the growing local church.

Another development was the Lunch Club started in 1970. Soon after the local committee was formed, a policy was developed to be more actively involved with the elderly. Coral Dunn, the parish worker encouraged Mary Middleton, a local mum, to run the club. Mary remembers: 'I used to pray that old people would come to the club, but when it opened and on the first day I was very disappointed when only three people turned up for dinner. Mind you, it was a very bad day — snow and ice everywhere. But I prayed that more would come. I knew that if God wanted this club here my prayer would be answered and thank God, when the weather started to get better more people started to come and during the summer I had fifty-three people for dinner on some days.' Mary continued to run the club five days a week until 1988 when she retired.

In September 1972, Bill Turner, who with Doreen his wife had been among the first group of leaders whom George Burton had trained in the Sunday Group was appointed senior youth leader. Bill was the first local person to become a member of staff.

Bill began his first full-time youth leader's appointment with a baptism of fire. Within weeks of his appointment, the club was overrun by a group of troublesome youngsters. For the next two years the pressures on Bill and his family were enormous. He had committed himself to the most difficult Mayflower appointment. The strain often showed. In 1973 Denis Downham left as warden and the Mayflower had almost a year's interregnum.

The long interregnum was a difficult time, particularly for the Turner family, and in 1974 Bill resigned. Doreen has written of that experience in her story. The lessons were painful. Had the vision failed? Were local people not really able to take on Christian leadership? Was it too soon?

Brian Seaman writes. 'When Denis and Edna moved to something more suited to their gifts — a parish near Liverpool — responsibility again passed to me as deputy warden. In seeking God's will for the wardenship the Council interviewed both Roger Sainsbury and Jenny and Marion and me. It was not just a question of which person was right for the job but what was the job? My own vision was the narrower one of concentrating on the life and growth of the local church?'

With Brian's move to Ladysmith Road, half a mile from the Centre, he had come away from the somewhat hothouse atmosphere of the Mayflower premises to a friendly terraced street. It was just an ordinary house in an ordinary street no different from the rest. From there, they really got to know the people of the area and settled to the pastoral work of building up the church. Brian remembers. 'Our next-door neighbours were Alan and Rita Dennis, two of George's Sunday Group leaders, whose friendship has meant a lot to us over the years. Over the road lived Pat Howell's aunt and later Jim and Janet Gosling moved round the corner. We were in good company. The area that I had felt too rough in my student days became home. In those days the East End spirit was very much alive; there was plenty of humour and vitality.'

Jack Wallace the chair of Mayflower Council from its earliest days wrote in the Mayflower *Log* that some of the local congregation were feeling that the original vision had been fulfilled in the existence of a local church as a bridgehead for Christ in Canning Town. Referring to Roland Allen's definition of a local church being self-supporting, self-propagating and self-governing, he recognized that Mayflower was none of these yet, or only in an embryonic way. Given the chance, Brian had argued, it could be all of these things if it was a smaller compact local church divorced from the untidy complex of clubs and buildings, financial worries and overburdened staff. There had in fact been a discussion on the Mayflower Council about dividing the work — asking the local borough council to take over the clubs, nursery etc., leaving the Mayflower church the sole responsibility of the warden and vicar.

However, the majority of the Mayflower Council believed the original vision was wider than that. They visualized Mayflower as becoming increasingly integrated into the life of Newham as a whole and also taking a leading part under the Bishop of Barking in the total life of the local churches. They also saw the possibility of expansion in numbers of staff members, and recognized Mayflower's potential as a unique training complex. The wider view was shared and fully represented by Roger and Jenny Sainsbury.

Before finally leaving the Downham era, it should be said that despite the difficulties Denis was deeply appreciated by many of the staff and residents. John Bourne writes:

Over the years I have read, often critically, of Denis Downham's time as warden. I was a resident during that period and owe a great deal to both him and Edna. During a lifetime you meet a small number of people who are very special and I regard Denis as being one such. He was a fine Bible teacher and a man with a great capacity to care and feel for people. To hear Denis preach on the great men and women of the Bible was a privilege. Looking retrospectively, I can see that both Denis and Brian saw a vision of the work contrary to most others of their time. I am sure, had Denis been warden or chaplain in more recent years, within the scope of the modern vision, his true self would have come through more fully.

...

Roger Sainsbury had been a curate at Christ Church, Spitalfields and for the previous twelve years had been warden of Shrewsbury House in Liverpool pioneering the rebuilding and reorganization of the centre and parish there. By the time of his arrival in September 1974, discussions had taken place about Mayflower's future. Rosemary Finch remembers Roger's arrival. 'I haven't come as Sainsbury the grocer. I've come as Sainsbury the builder, and build I will.'

The buildings were now over forty years old, built in a different era. Some liked the halls with their maze of corridors and club rooms. In particular George Burton had felt there was real value in getting teenagers involved in doing up old club rooms. 'We won their friendship and respect and they even voluntarily contributed money towards the materials. If you provide them with a brand new club room with expensive equipment they will simply come in, make off with what they can and smash the rest.' But generally it was recognized that the buildings needed a major revamp.

A working-party report was later to describe the buildings as:

. . . the siege mentality of the middle-class church defensively placed in hostile territory. From the outside they are forbidding; locked doors and shuttered windows are psychological as well as physical barriers. Inside, the Centre is a maze, with no feeling of corporate identity. Only in the tudor-style courtyard is there any idea of 'place' but this rather escapist atmosphere seems unrelated to Mayflower's drive and purpose. Mayflower is large: the site is more than an acre in area and the buildings contain about 50,000 square feet of space. With the replacement of the overcrowded homes of Canning Town by new flats, these buildings make Mayflower appear worn out, shabby and unwelcoming: a poor advertisement for the cause they uphold.[1]

At an extraordinary meeting of the Mayflower Council in December 1974, it was decided that the whole complex must be redeveloped together. This was very much in line with the wider vision that Mayflower Council had adopted in appointing Roger Sainsbury. He wrote in the first Mayflower *log* after his arrival: 'Consciously we are now looking towards the '80s, realizing that big decisions have to be made about the future.'

Roger published a book entitled *Towards 1984*. The message of the book was that in a rapidly changing world, Christians must take the risk not only of a church with 'open doors' but of an open church. The church needed to fight against a 'closed shop' appearance to the world and plan open structures, but at the same time encourage commitment to a Lord concerned for all of life and not just the religious.

In particular this meant encouraging Christians to get involved in community action through local tenants' groups and residents' associations rather than forming exclusive church community action groups. The sociological group they belonged to was their street or their block of flats, not the church. This approach had implications for the buildings, for staffing, for Mayflower's place in its local community and for the very nature of what Mayflower was.

A redevelopment working party was set up by the Mayflower Council. It had nine members, two of whom were local church members, the others drawn from the British Council of Churches, Frontier Youth Trust and the Deanery Pastoral Committee. It was chaired by Ted Roberts who was vicar of St James-the-Less, Bethnal Green.

The report of the working party runs to thirty pages and speaks very little of the bringing of people to faith in Christ or of building an indigenous church. It recognized that Mayflower had been relatively independent and autonomous though co-operating with other Christian bodies and other agencies.

Now that Mayflower has taken root it would seem that the opportunity exists to work within a wider context. The case for co-operation between different Christian churches and groups and between these people and social agencies is a powerful one. Only by involving themselves in community life can Christians hope to influence any but their own committed gatherings: only by coming together and acting corporately can this influence have sufficient strength . . .[2]

Suggestions were made about future staffing including a detached youth worker and a family case worker. Roger himself was keen on the appointment of a community chaplain to work with the other churches, the borough and the Canning Town Community Development Project. Colin Watts became a Labour councillor and Roger himself became an alderman developing a close relationship with Newham Borough Council.

The working party had suggested that Mayflower needed to decide what it was. Should it concentrate on building up a local, worshipping congregation as an independent evangelical/interdenominational centre. Alternatively should it decide to move closer to the Church of England as an Anglican parish centre or an ecumenical centre or should it concentrate on being a training centre or a Christian social centre.

This broader context was very much at the heart of the redevelopment of the buildings. 'Our new plant should be such as to suit our new vision of God's mission and not control or restrict it,' the original motion had said. Roger Sainsbury had spelt out five things he disliked about the buildings. 'There was no inviting entrance, the Youth Club building was totally unsuitable for present day youth work, there was no lounge for informal Church activities, accommodation for long term residents like teachers, social workers etc. was not provided and the Mayflower garden needed opening up to the community.'

It was decided to go ahead with redevelopment in phases involving a new youth club, the conversion of the swimming pool to a dry Sports Hall, the redevelopment of Cooper Street hostel block into a training centre, the redevelopment of the chapel building with a central auditorium and craft exhibition areas, the development of the ground floor of the Vincent Street building into a day centre for the elderly, including a large dining hall, lounge, welfare advice office and reception, and the upper floors into administrative offices and staff accommodation.

An architectural competition was organized which was won by Stillman, Eastwick Field. Partnerships were forged with Newham Borough Council and the Sports Council for funding the different buildings and appeal documents were prepared and dispatched. The original estimate had been £600,000 but this rose to £870,000 and finally to £1 million. The conversion of the hostel into a training centre and the chapel conversion had to be abandoned because of the rising cost of the rest of the redevelopment.

But the old contradictions wouldn't go away. How did the local church fit into the picture? The working party was deliberately aimed wider and included only two local church members. Negotiations with the borough were complex and relied heavily on Roger's own contacts and skills. The Appeal committee and the Redevelopment committee needed to rely heavily on outside expertise rather than local knowledge. One local couple who had given a great deal of themselves over the years argued that if others wanted to come from outside and build an adult centre that was OK, but please don't expect the local people to run it. Colin Watts 'felt that the focus and the effect so vehemently targeted in those early years was now being harnessed into new buildings of bricks and mortar and not to building a local "church" of local people.'

Questions were raised at Mayflower Council about

turning the swimming bath into a Sports Hall. As a main Mayflower objective was to reach people for Jesus, could this be done in a government-supported/staffed organization? John Bourne remembers in 1977 when the redevelopment programme was well under way meeting a husband and wife who had been residents in early Mayflower days.

They were intelligent people who saw things very clearly. In a discussion that followed, they questioned the Mayflower redevelopment programme; they questioned the Mayflower vision; they questioned everything that I and so many others believed and held as being important. They questioned whether the youth work had really found a way of presenting the gospel to young city people. They questioned why Christians from outside the area should financially support the work that could otherwise be provided by the local council. They questioned how you could expect a large active church to support and run such a centre as the Mayflower let alone a small city church. They bombarded me with questions I had never heard before. I realized I couldn't answer them and went away shell-shocked. I never again saw the Mayflower in the same light. My vision of the work had been turned upside down.

• • •

For a number of local leaders and potential leaders the tensions became too great and a number left the church. These included Alan and Rita Dennis, Pat and Len Howell from the original Sunday Group as well as Colin and Mary Watts and a number of others. It wasn't an organized exodus but happened over a number of months. There was a recognition that all was not well with their Christian lives both inside and outside Mayflower. Some formed a house church which still meets in Plaistow. It was a difficult time. Those who left often spoke of the release they found from the demands of the Mayflower and the spiritual growth that resulted.

But this was a distinct loss. Apart from Jim and Janet Gosling, all the remaining group of people who had been nurtured for local leadership and who were still in their thirties had now gone. There were a number of older local people who could take additional responsibility and indeed did through the pastoral assistants' training that was run by Roy Trevivian and Jim Gosling, but inevitably their time span of active involvement was limited.

Did this represent a failure of the original vision — an indigenous church? To some extent, but added to the tensions already outlined was the fact that all the people who left Mayflower had already moved out of Canning Town to Plaistow and East Ham. David Sheppard and George Burton had encouraged the Sunday Group members to stay locally and the housing association had helped. Rita Dennis felt they had fulfilled that vision. She voiced what a number felt.

We stayed in this area when everyone else left. We believed God wanted us here. We believed that God would look after us – and he has. Nobody in their right mind allows their children to go to a local school. No minister does. I used to get so angry because people used to come down in this area to do work and serve the people but they weren't prepared to put their children's education at risk. We believed that God would look after our children. I believe our daughter Karen has paid a price for us being Christians and our involvement with Mayflower. But she's an intellligent girl, she's got a job, she's been to college and our son went to university. God has been really good to us.'

...

But Newham like the rest of London is a series of villages. The ethos of Canning Town is very different from other parts of the borough. Until recently if you wanted to buy your own house you had to look elsewhere — there was no owner occupation in Canning Town. How local is local? People travel some distance to attend church but Canning Town remains a fairly self-contained community accentuated by the major rivers and roads that cut it off from elsewhere. With the move out of the immediate area, members of the group had left a Canning Town mentality and a Mayflower claustrophobia which had been a release but never found a new home in Christian terms outside the safe confines of their own group. They were caught in a limbo. In later years, when the emphasis at Mayflower reverted to building a local church, some felt they couldn't return because being strong characters the emerging church couldn't cope with them. On the other hand, the experience of church life at Mayflower had perhaps discouraged them from the struggle of getting actively involved in another church. In some ways the house group is a re-creation of what Mayflower might have been but without a wider context it is in danger of suffocating itself.

Meanwhile the remodelled buildings were taking shape and additional staff were being recruited. One of these was Roy Trevivian. He had originally trained as a Methodist minister and had worked for a number of years with the BBC. The appointment was risky. Roy had suffered from depression and had had a breakdown and a drink problem. Mark Birchall remembers his interview for the post of chaplain.

He lay back in a vast armchair, chain-smoking; none of the interviewing group smoked – we all secretly thought it was a dirty and dangerous habit, something no proper Christian ought to do. But most of us were occasional drinkers, while Roy, having seen the damage drink had done in families he had known well, regarded drink as a prime enemy and could not understand how apparently committed Christians could think it was acceptable. Nonetheless, we appointed him: he came – and did an amazing job at Mayflower. He began his time with us by taking a part-time job as milkman to get to know people and be known, to soak himself in the local culture.

. . .

Roy's first love was evangelism and he began his time at Mayflower by visiting a thousand houses in the neighbourhood with questionnaires about life and Jesus. He too found a hardness of response. 'The picture is pretty black, but to know that, to face that and wrestle with it, is far better in the long run than living in cloud-cuckoo-land.'

No one was neutral about Roy. 'The fact that Christians have problems too and need not cover them up or be ashamed — I thank Roy Trevivian for this,' said one resident. On the other hand, another found him 'unsupportive, unhelpful, unloving, vain, arrogant and on occasions rude and spiritually destructive.'

Rich Gerard wrote of Roy.

There is a notice in the former counselling room at the Mayflower. It shows a drawing of a tower block and says, 'If you feel like jumping, see Roy first and he will jump with you.' Roy Trevivian spent a lot of time with a lot of people in that room. He talked to many types – alcoholics, drug addicts, depressives, people with marital problems, single mums and so on. That simple notice was a demonstration of Roy's ability to defuse his visitors' tension and to meet people where they were at.

Yet empathy and understanding are typical of all Roy's relationships, coupled with his uninhibited naturalness, whether he be cupping the Queen Mother's hand in both of his like a Dutch uncle or having a quick puff with some of our women before going into the evening service.

I am sure that Roy would readily discount all of these gifts to emphasize that this warmth and understanding are a reflection of his love of Jesus.[3]

There was a great sense of loss when Roy had a heart attack and then a severe stroke in 1980 which took him away from Mayflower.

Two additional experienced youth workers joined Pip Wilson the senior youth leader to take plans forward in the new youth club building. A Sports Hall manager was appointed. With these Rich Gerard came onto the staff as community worker — a local church member and former docker who had given many years to Mayflower.

The major redevelopment, the appeal for money, the wider partnership — all helped to make Mayflower 'high profile' again. The *Log* now transformed into *Mayflower News* became a regular insert in the *Church of England Newspaper* and sometimes in the *Church Times*. The Youth Reports were distributed to the Borough Youth and Education Departments as well as outside supporters. The Queen Mother opened the new club building and the Archbishop of Canterbury, the revamped community buildings and Sports Hall. Roy Trevivian's contacts in television and radio ensured a number of programmes. Central Television did a programme based on Pip Wilson's insights into the youth work. Ronald Allison advised on publicity and public relations.

The appeal went to Mayflower supporters, charitable trusts and foundations, to the City, to commerce and industry and to the wider public. Money came in and in April 1981, a month before the final celebration, Mark Birchall could write. 'We have been constantly reminded of the Lord's goodness by the way funds have come precisely at the right time to meet bills, and we have only had to borrow a relatively small sum from the bank in the last few months. Half the total given so far has come in amounts of less than £1,000 — from many hundreds of individuals to whom we are deeply grateful.'[4] Of the £1 million needed half came from the public sector and half from trusts, churches and individuals. The new buildings had triumphantly met the criterion of opening the Centre up to the community. They were welcoming, spacious, convenient and the garden was no longer hidden away from public view.

The partnership with the borough was strengthened. In effect it meant that they would not build another youth centre in the area but would see Mayflower as providing for the youth of the local community. The same would be true of the day centre, although no formal agreements were drawn up. In addition to the contribution to the buildings, the borough also paid the majority of two youth workers' salaries and took over the funding of the third when the Urban Aid Grant expired, paying towards the Sports Hall manager's salary and a substantial community work grant covering salary and overheads.

The youth team benefited from the availability of borough-run courses and contact with social services. But there was a warning light. The nursery school which had been running since Dockland Settlement days was an integral part of the Mayflower work. Despite the grants from the local authority and the Department of Education there were increasing deficits which had to be met out of Mayflower funds. There was also a cash flow problem as expenses were paid before reimbursement was received. The initial proposal was that Mayflower should link up with St Luke's Primary School which had a nursery class. If this happened, Mayflower nursery would become a voluntary-aided school at only a small annual cost to Mayflower. This idea was favoured by the diocese. It was, however, felt that Mayflower would no longer have a majority voice on the board of managers while the school itself would become only an annexe to St Luke's School. As an alternative, it was agreed to pursue negotiations with the borough Education Department to hand over the financial responsibility on the understanding that Mayflower must retain a majority on any future board of management. It was put to the borough that unless it took this responsibility the school would probably close.

The borough agreed to take over financial responsibility but insisted on majority control of the managing body. On this being challenged, the reply was, '. . . this may be taken as the Education Committee's offer which is not negotiable.' In the face of this, Mayflower Council felt at least it was essential that the preservation of Christian instruction be included in the agreement. This never happened and the school was transferred.

Initially, recruitment of both teaching and nursery nurse staff was done without difficulty and Christian personnel were appointed. Inevitably, however, on Betty Bradley's retirement as head teacher with the new head being appointed by the Education Department from a short list of three names submitted by the managers, there was no protection for Mayflower interests. In the event, Georgina Mepham was appointed in 1987.

There were undoubted advantages in the transfer. Apart from lifting the financial burden, the head teacher was integrated into the borough system instead of being rather isolated as the only direct grant school in the borough. In particular, this ensured a ready availability of supply teachers. Over the years the buildings have been redeveloped and added to by the borough to maintain them in excellent condition.

Georgina has developed the school excellently. She has given a hundred per cent commitment to the work and there is a very good working relationship with Mayflower. There is no doubt, however, that the school is totally independent of Mayflower Family Centre and is not run as a Christian school.

By accepting substantial funding from the borough in

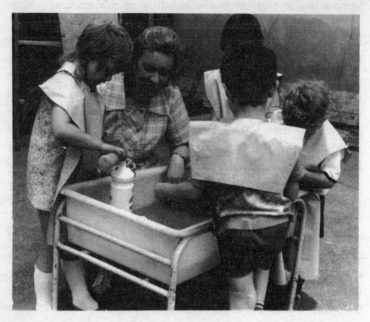

Betty Bradley, Head of Mayflower Nursery School

other areas of the work Mayflower took on a clear obligation to meet borough criteria, the classic problem of serving two masters, and this had repercussions later on.

Setting Mayflower in a wider context did not only embrace partnership with the borough. There were many discussions about joining with St Luke's in a general redevelopment as a parish centre and the formation of a formal Anglican Team Ministry south of the Newham Way. Mayflower youth work recognized the wider Frontier Youth Trust context of its work. A separate management committee was formed with representatives of the diocese, FYT and the borough as well as the Mayflower Council and the church members of the youth work team would serve on this. It was hoped that this would give local leaders a real say under the overall leadership and guidance of the senior youth worker in the running of the work.

The need for Christians from other areas to get vision, inspiration and training in urban situations for ministry, youth and community work was felt to be as great if not greater than ever before. Mayflower with its fifteen years' experience was in a unique position to do this, particularly now that there were more local Christians active in the church and the community. There was a cutback in the number of resident places to six in the redeveloped buildings and a formalization of their stay to two years. But alongside this, ideas for using the Cooper Street building as an Urban Training Centre were developed. This would be run by a committee drawn from national Christian and other agencies involved in urban ministry and training as well as local representatives. Finally, the Sports Hall was seen as a local community facility open to all groups and individuals which might develop its own committee drawn from users and the local community.

This partnership approach would open Mayflower up more, there would be greater Christian and secular expertise appropriate for each area of work and make it more accountable. It would relieve the emerging local church from responsibility for the wider work and yet give them some say through their representatives on the different committees.

Again there was an early-warning note. The first manager of the new Sports Hall was not a Christian and he had resigned fairly soon after his appointment. Mayflower Council in considering a replacement felt he or she should be a practising Christian as part of the Mayflower senior staff, even though the role of the Sports Hall was not specifically Christian-orientated. In an eagerness to meet the ongoing needs of the area or get a particular project off the ground, there is always a temptation to go for what seems to produce the greatest practical benefit. This often

A Different Kind of Church

involves appointing people with enthusiasm and expertise but with little if any Christian conviction. It is justified on the grounds that they will be influenced towards Christianity by the rest of the team. Usually the reverse is the case. Many Christian organizations have done this and have moved away from a biblically-based mission so that in the end the Christian content is reduced to a general desire to do good to others.

As Mayflower entered the 1980s it did so with a new set of buildings, a strong staff team and developing partnerships in the borough and wider church. A number of the contradictions remained, however, and were to surface again in the next decade.

How to Get Up After a Fall
Johnny Ringwood

It was in 1967 when I began my walk with the Lord. I lived in the then notorious Manor Road buildings.

I met this fella called Bobby Halsey, a typical streetwise sort of a man. I took to him straightaway, he lived just around the corner from me.

One night I called in on him, and there was quite a lot of people in his front room. I got the shock of my life when I heard the conversation – it was full of Alleluias, Amens, and Jesus. I quickly became a metal worker and made a bolt for the door. It did not add up; how come a man like Bobby could be one of these Christians? He did not fit the mould, or not at least how I imagined a Christian would be.

I was going through a pretty rough period at this time. I was suffering from very severe depressions and some cockeyed panic attacks. What was most ironic – there did not appear to be any rationale to it. I was blessed with a lovely wife, Brenda, and two fine young sons, Terry and Steve. I had a good job. I seemed to have it all sown up, but I did not have any peace.

So I was ripe for Bobby when he started to talk to me about Jesus and the promised peace. I guess I had always been searching for something. So one night I gave myself to the Lord.

It appears that the meetings in Bob's house were a House Group from the Mayflower. It was a hot summer evening when I first came through the doors of the Mayflower. I was wearing a black, pinstripe, three-piece suit. That's how I remembered going to church, you wore your Sunday best. Now remember this was in the sixties, the time of the flower power and beads etc.; to say the dress of the youngsters in the congregation was casual was to put it mildly. It did not take me long to get in the swing.

I remember my conversion as a really lovely time, it lasted at least three months. During this time I just loved everybody and drove most of them crackers. I just wanted them to share this wonderful feeling.

My first association with the buildings now called the Mayflower was in the war. It was then called the Dockland Settlement. I had spent a lot of time in the large communal air-raid shelter in Beckton Road park, this was during the Blitz. Along with many others I caught scabies, the Dockland Settlement was one of the only places that had a bath, so I used to be brought there. They would give me a good scrub, then paint me pink with Calamine lotion.

The next contact I had was when I was eleven, the Dockland, (that's what we called it) had a terrific boxing club run by a very good trainer called Blacky. Then there was this long gap till 1967 when my real life started.

I find it very difficult to put what happened all those years in neat little packages. Of course David Sheppard and Grace featured very strongly and so did Brian Seaman, the curate at that time. I remember him visiting me in hospital. We also had a lot of young people staying at the Mayflower at that time, we called them 'resis' short for residents. They came from all over the place, even as far as Australia.

I remember the Searcher Groups. These were especially for people who had just found the Lord or were still searching. I was really on fire at this time, and praying to God to find me some Christian

Johnny Ringwood

work to do but it did not happen. I lapsed for a period around the time Denis Downham came, so I don't really know too much about him.

I started coming back on a regular basis when Roger Sainsbury and Roy Trevivian came to the Mayflower; it was during their period that a great deal of new building work took place. I remember calling in one day when Roger asked could I have a word with him. He asked could I have a word with Roy as he was suffering a very bad depression bout. I thought this was a bit strange, a reversal of role; did not vicars normally adopt this counselling-type role?

Roy was a wonderful man. I always take to someone when their eyes fill with tears when they hear something sad. Roy's heart was always on his sleeve. He came to us a fairly broken man, he had just left the BBC where he was a producer in the religious broadcasting department. I grew to love Roy especially after he suffered a cruel and disabling stroke. He was a wonderful influence on my life and since he died I miss him a lot . . .

I remember a conversation with Roy, it was one Tuesday night in 1976; he was a shrewd old boy. He said 'Johnny, do you know the Kray twins?' I said I know of them but I did not know them personally. He then said, 'Do you ever get up to any mischief?' Now for a while I had been pushing a little bit of stolen goods. Now remember that I was supposedly a Christian and Roy had obviously heard about it. I remember now actually being a bit boastful about it. On the following Saturday I had a visit from the police, they searched my house and found a quantity of stolen goods. It appears someone in the square had rung them and told them of my activities. To cut a long story short, I went to court and was sentenced.

Don't try and con God, it don't work. If you say you are a Christian you had better be one. I was sent down on the 23rd December. To say I was sorry was to put it mildly. I had let everyone down, but most of all I had betrayed the Lord. So I prayed, oh, how I prayed. After a couple of weeks I was sent to an open prison. My wife Brenda was really fighting to get me released. She and many others thought the sentence was a bit severe considering it was my first offence. Funnily enough I did not. I truly believed this was God punishing me for letting Him down.

I was very glad, however, when the appeal court judges agreed with Brenda and set me free after just two months. That two months were truly the worst of my life.

What's all this to do with the Mayflower? Well when I came out, the Lord at last answered my prayer about giving me a job. I am a qualified weight-training instructor; Pip Wilson who was then the youth leader in our club heard about this and offered me a job as an instructor, so I spent the next couple of years not only training young men in weightlifting, but also spent a lot of time sharing my experiences and telling them that even a shrewd old boy like me could not beat the system.

The years sped by and probably the nicest show of love and

forgiveness was when the congregation elected me as their chairman. The Lord has been very patient. If I was God I would have chucked me out years ago.

Canning Town – 1960s

6

Exciting, Difficult Days

(1970-1985)

WHEN GEORGE BURTON died in 1966 it was difficult to replace him. A number of leaders came for periods, but did not stay long. The combined demands of youth work, community life and relationships with local people were difficult. Rosemary Finch was now on the staff, there were still a lot of residents and the pattern of open youth clubs with smaller groups was maintained. The aims, objectives and structures set up in George Burton's day, changed very little until 1975.

The work went through periods of real growth when there was stable leadership. Young Christians came forward from Sunday Night Group and Group 69 and there was local leadership in the groups though the open youth work was still very dependent on residents.

What about the problems of the 'unclubable' youngsters? Paradoxically a local person can have extra pressures. Bill Turner from the original Sunday Group and appointed senior youth leader in 1972 had to deal with the same area and tenement block where he himself had been brought up. To reject those youngsters would have been to reject his own roots and people. When a new appointment is made or a new building opened the local young people will test the person or the situation to the limit. John Bourne remembers.

Within weeks of Bill taking responsibility, the club was overrun by a group of young people. Some of these members dominated the next six to eight years of club life. Within three months the club was in retreat. Open club was temporarily closed and on reopening struggled under great difficulties . . . Because of the demands on the youth leaders, much of the group work, particularly with young Christians was stopped or reduced in scope. The long-established club talk was suspended and much of the good work of the previous years was destroyed. It was a long hard year that on occasions demanded police assistance and first-aid for the leaders. The pressures built up on Bill and his family. In July 1974 he resigned. It was a sad end to his leadership. I do not feel that the pressures that Bill was under allowed him to appreciate the high regard with which he was held by those with whom he worked the closest.

* * *

When Roger Sainsbury succeeded Denis Downham he brought with him his experience as warden of Shrewsbury House, Liverpool, another of the founding units of FYT. Roger had been an FYT committee member from its earliest days. Pip Wilson followed Roger south and became senior youth leader in February 1975.

Pip came from St Helen's in Lancashire where he had gained long experience and a reputation as a good leader. The testing of the new leader was repeated. John Bourne remembers.

Within days of entering the post. Pip had to confront the same youngsters who had caused so much trouble in Bill's day. To this were added emerging new groups such as the Tramps and the Minnis . . . It was a very difficult time. This time was a watershed in the youth work history. That momentum set up in George Burton's era had now run out and future leadership would have to establish its own direction and structure.

Pip brought about changes, regained help from some of the local church members and re-estanblished the Christian outreach of the work. The club became much more professional in its approach. Kris Traer, Doug McWilliam and Geoff Flynn all served as full-time youth workers. Youth work assistants were also appointed. Pip worked hard. For every four steps he took forward he was pushed three back. He must rarely have relaxed but the Christmas term of 1977 is one that remains clearly in my mind. Throughout that term, not one youngster was fined or banned from the club. On the last evening of term, Trevor Brooking, the West Ham and England footballer presented competition prizes to the club members – the evening must have given Pip a sense of satisfaction and reward for three years' hard work.

· · ·

Pip Wilson has written about his experiences in a book *Gutter Feelings*. Doug McWilliam wrote about him.

Pip often gave the impression of being solid and dependable, but beneath there is a very sensitive fragile person. The fragility revealed itself in a burst of anger at the injustice surrounding our work. The kids who were hurting were taken on board creating more hurt. The very struggle to affirm the meanest, hardest of the bunch was often like a candle flickering in the dark, with a gale blowing around.

I think Jesus had the gift of affirmation. Pip uniquely also has this gift. There are not many people who have come into contact with him and not been blessed by the meeting. But Pip's gift of affirmation has caused some of the deepest pain because it means taking on the worst. Vulnerable, open, generous, yet fragile and weak, very committed to the Kingdom theology of Jesus whose desire is to bring wholeness in unwhole people, to value the devalued – Pip is uniquely unique.[1]

· · ·

The greater professionalism of the youth work was linked with funding. The local authority was more on its feet in terms of what was expected from places that were given grants. It was developing its own youth service and running clubs. Training courses were being set up which workers from across the borough could attend and benefit from. The borough encouraged the establishment of a youth work management committee which would oversee that particular side of the work with borough and other youth work representatives to provide support and responsibility for club management. This was part of the need for accountability for the use of public funds. Regular reports were written by members of the youth work team and others associated with the work. These were headed, Confidential and were distributed to the borough Youth and Education Department, the Mayflower Council, the Chapel committee and supporters of the work outside.

Along with these developments there was a change in the local community which was reflected in club work. Unemployment was rising fast. Previously most club members over fifteen had jobs or an apprenticeship which made them more positive in their outlook on life. Now many of them would have nothing to do all day, would drift around becoming increasingly bored and alienated. Disruptive and violent youngsters had as good as destroyed the club. Workers were feeling battered. Pip Wilson started one of his youth work reports:

There was a lot of violence in the air tonight. Again, it's hours of talk about the remembrances of 'the chase' or 'the bashing' given and received at football matches. Jacko is known to be 'mad' at football matches. This Saturday he said, 'Was the first match I've ever been in the ground — I usually hang around and watch for the stragglers and bash them.' X threw a petrol bomb and everyone was pleased that it made the *News of the World*, page two, they said. It seemed one of them had phoned the paper and claimed responsibility — the ICF (Inner City Firm) is what they call the gang. Jacko is just in club again following a week's suspension for violence when we received a visiting team here in the club. In such a body, one carries a hammer in his sports bag, another a rounders bat — knives are around at the moment. I could go on — but it does make you sick and we have to live with it — so share it we must.[2]

Church and local leaders Jim and Janet Gosling spoke of the paid staff not seeing eye to eye with locals who were seen as 'enthusiastic amateurs'. Alan Dennis says:

I feel we'd been there a long time and in a sense holding the fort while a lot of people were coming and going. We gained quite a lot of experience. Not just me, but lots of others. It was actually said to me, 'We are paid staff, you're not. We're the professionals, we've been trained.' Although I'd been doing youth work for somewhere in the region of fifteen years by that stage. I'd had a set of keys to Mayflower, for twenty years and they took them away because I wasn't paid staff.'

In the end the issue was put to Alan in a formal letter.

'I was so emtionally charged by it that I went into the church, got on my knees and prayed about it. I felt very clearly that God was saying you can't go any further while you're here. I came home and said I think it's time we left. And so we did, which wasn't easy. It was our life.'

...

On the other hand, the staff members felt isolated and unsupported. Doug McWilliam expressed his feelings following a staff visit to a leadership week run by Evangelical Alliance.

Having spent a week at the Evangelical Alliance Conference during the beginning of October it seemed so distant and unattached from the reality of what we in the inner city of Canning Town are trying to do.

Does the Church just not understand what is going on in the inner cities of this country? How can an organisation such as Evangelical Alliance stand up and declare itself for the Kingdom when people are crying out in the cities. Christians are becoming numb from giving so much, they are absorbing the culture of the oppressed and feel nobody understands. I often come away from the club and sit and listen to people talk about what they are doing in their churches, how God is blessing them, and yet I feel inside how often people do not understand what it means to be in a place like Canning Town. The needs we have here as tried, battered inner-city workers have largely gone unmentioned. [3]

• • •

One way to help that sense of isolation was through the youth work reports. They told what was happening in the club, the good things, the bad things and gave many personal views of the work and the area. They helped youth team members express the feelings they had. Supporters used to write in with letters of encouragement which were much appreciated.

But the reports sometimes had a different effect in Canning Town. John Bourne who was on the Youth Work Management committee has written. 'The reports often took a very negative view of the area and represented it in a bad light in order to boost the importance and difficulties of the work. A Mayflower supporter in Eastbourne had access to reports that were denied the people of Canning Town. These reports often caused a reaction from the borough education and other departments and were deeply resented by a number of church members and local people who did have access to them.'

When a gulf grew between the youth work and the local church, the reports had played their part in creating the difficulties. Rosemary Finch also on the committee commented. 'To a certain extent Pip's reports used to major on the bad kids — the most dramatic. Where are the average kids? You're talking about the disadvantaged all the time but there must be some young people who would like to come in . . . The church people said they wouldn't send their kids if that is what was going on and they wouldn't have anything to do with the young people there.'

The youth team was aware of this problem. There were teenagers who were relaxed, pleasant, friendly and enjoyed friendships and club facilities, but increasingly they were deterred by the more aggressive boys.

Pip was keen to involve local people in the work and a number were brought in, being paid on a sessional basis. This was positive and there was a very strong commitment to the team and to one another. This was fostered by youth team weekends together and other training sessions which built close relationships. Apart from the residents, however, practically none of these had any other involvement with Mayflower, particularly with the Mayflower church.

In the face of these trends it was natural that the youth team should look to Frontier Youth Trust which Mayflower played a major part in establishing for support and training. The links between FYT and Mayflower are too numerous to list. Most of the key youth workers of the 1970s and 1980s played an important role in FYT. Philip Thompson, FYT's first chair coordinated the redevelopment of Mayflower buildings. Roger Sainsbury subsequently became chair of FYT trustees. Pip Wilson became vice-chair. Jack Wallace chaired a conference in 1978 organized by Roger Sainsbury and Michael Eastman which gave rise in 1980 to the formation of the Evangelical Coalition for Urban Mission (ECUM), the founding partners of which are FYT, the Evangelical Urban Training Project, Christians in Industrial Areas and the Inner City Group of Shaftesbury Project (now Christian Impact). Margaret Starns who was secretary/administrator at Mayflower from 1969—1975 became FYT's administrative officer in 1976 and is still going strong there!

FYT through Michael Eastman played a part in the redevelopment of the building. He sat on the working party which rethought the whole plant and drew up the brief for the architectural competition.

The youth club premises were brilliantly designed to give expression to youth work principles in bricks and mortar. Many people came to see and learn from this.

Mayflower was also used for some FYT training events and the team made a significant impact on the life and work of FYT including the Training the Trainers programme as well as the national conferences and London-wide events where a thirty-strong Mayflower contingent would make its presence felt.

FYT provided a place where the youth team could share, could feel that others were experiencing similar pressures and could learn together. The difficulty this posed locally was that the direction and philosophy of the youth work was felt not to be determined by the Mayflower Council, the Chapel committee or even the Youth Work Management committee but by FYT workers and associates who didn't live in Canning Town. There was also the feeling that sharing the Good News of Jesus Christ was not a high priority.

John Bourne felt that during his time as a club leader, '. . . most of the information and training from FYT was geared to the theories of youth work and social awareness, all very valuable, but not to the nitty gritty business of preaching the gospel.' He remembered a visit by club leaders to All Souls Club in Central London. 'During discussions one of their leaders expressed concern about their lack of success in bringing youngsters to Christ and questioned whether it was possible to give an effective message within the structure of an open club.

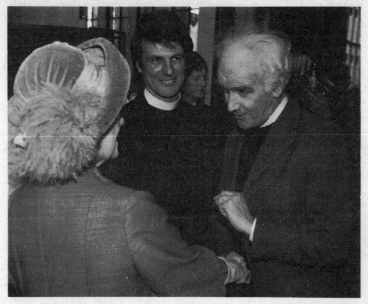

Roy Trevivian greets the Queen Mother with Roger Sainsbury – opening of Club 1980

There was a real desire by all the full-time youth workers and the residents to see people become Christians and an active looking for opportunities to share their faith. The experience of the past was that open clubs were not a fruitful place for this. It had been the group work, the spending of so much time with a small number which had brought results. There were attempts to work with small groups in the late '70s and '80s. But in general it was more difficult – youth leaders had families and couldn't open their homes in the way George Burton had.

Alongside the regular youth work there was a desire to do something more specific in the face of rising unemployment. By January 1976, the percentage rate among males was 9.5 per cent compared to the Greater London rate of 5.4 per cent. The Canning Town exchange area was one of the four worst black spots for male unemployment in London, along with Poplar, Stepney and Holloway.

Roger Sainsbury spearheaded a number of responses. On a Mayflower initiative, the boroughs of Tower Hamlets and Newham applied for a Community Industry scheme to employ one hundred people. One of the bases for this was at Mayflower. Two Mayflower men, George Tilley and Doug McWilliam were employed as team consultants. Roger became chairman of Newham and Tower Hamlets Job Creation Programme to provide short-term jobs of social value. As part of this, Mayflower sponsored a Youth and Community Work Assistants Project creating nine jobs for young adults to work in four youth centres in the area, plus one worker, John Oliver to coordinate the scheme. The tasks undertaken were general youth-club work — running coffee bars, craft groups, literacy work with immigrants, work with under fives, administration, work with community groups and running sports teams. John ran training sessions for the group. Although the emphasis was on creating jobs, it was felt that workers needed a first experience in which they could begin to understand what jobs they could do and in what areas they could develop their skills and abilities. Of those who worked on this project, one is now a lecturer at a youth work college, another a probation worker and one works for Scripture Union.

Another new project was the Newham City Farm for twenty-one workers. There were four skilled project leaders and the rest were unemployed young people including three who were mentally handicapped. City Farms involved animals and gardening in small plots of land in cities that would otherwise stand idle, wasted or rubbish-strewn. The farms are not necessarily self-supporting in terms of produce. They do, however, give children and adults in urban areas a first-hand experience of rural activities.

Trevor Lawson was appointed project officer to Mayflower to coordinate this development. A site in Docklands at Beckton was secured from the Port of London Authority and the project began. For a while the City Farm had an annexe at Mayflower with chickens and rabbits running around the garden. Only the wages for the project came from the Job Creation Programme, all materials and animals coming from gifts and donations. The Farm was officially opened by Princess Anne in July 1977. Newham borough could not at the time afford to sponsor the project, but it was a long-term success and was handed over to the borough in 1979 and is still bringing pleasure to many people and providing a few long-term jobs.

Another brainchild of Trevor Lawson's was the building of a ferro-cement forty foot ketch in a disused shed at the North Thames Gas works at Bromley-by-Bow. The project involved fifteen unemployed young people initially under the Job Creation Programme and then the Youth Opportunities Programme. It hit a number of problems, partly due to change in government programmes, partly to the need to shift sites and to frequent burglaries which left the team with virtually no proper tools. It took a long time to build, and at times morale was very low. But in the end hundreds of youngsters had experienced their one year of work on it, learning skills like carpentry, plumbing, engineering and electronics. The boat was named the *Cockney Spirit* and was handed over on completion by Mayflower to a new Cockney Spirit Trust of which Pip Wilson is the chair and Joy Sansom, an ex-resident, youth worker/secretary at Mayflower, is secretary. The boat is now used on the Essex coast by youth and other groups for weekends and other trips.

By the end of 1981 when Roger left, Mayflower itself was employing thirty-eight people full and part time. This included several young people, mostly unemployed school-leavers, who had been made available through Community Industry or YOP schemes. They were serving in reception, in the kitchen, in the youth club, in the office and one young man was in the maintenance team.

The pressure of unemployment was seen most clearly in youth club members. Having nothing to do, nowhere to go, coping with the constant feeling of rejection and the endless search for non-existent jobs had serious effects on the development of young people. The youth work team felt that although the purpose-built club was intended to run as an evening provision to meet the needs of young people during their free time after school or work, they needed to look at daytime provision for those who had whole days free. So Day Space was born, initially one day a week for two hours, but then expanding to three days. Doug McWilliam coordinated this and worked it in with a community programme. This initially involved two full-time workers, collating jobs and information, one with an emphasis on girls and young women, and four part-time posts, a minibus driver, a cleaner, someone overseeing toy-making in the workshop space in the club and a finance clerk. Hanson Raffo and Sharon Clerk, two young members of Senior Club whom Doug had been working with for some time took two of the posts.

They opened at midday because many young people tend to sleep in. They tried to create a different atmosphere from Senior Club, a quiet atmosphere for discussion, showing films, low music and a finishing time of 3.00 p.m. Doug describes what was on offer:

It offers:

Information on jobs
Help with legal advice

Advice on training, job opportunities and further education
Social skills and life skills training

In 1983 we were able to commence a community programme
funded by the Manpower Services Commission (MSC). This enabled
us to employ four part-time and two full-time workers. Apart from
MSC money for these workers, we received no financing of any kind.
Any financial outgoings were to be absorbed by the club. We were
able from the outset of the project to initiate a job-search programme.
We established good regular contacts both with the local Job Centre
and Careers Service.

The local Careers Office had just appointed an outreach team and
they were invited to come into the project to give advice and to see
what was going on within it. The outcome of this was Careers
sending one of their officers on a regular basis into the project with
a current list of job vacancies. This was to prove a major step forward.
Many of the young people using Day Space have been long-term
unemployed, their unemployment ranging from one year to six years,
two or three having only ever worked for six or seven weeks. Part
of what we try to do within the project is to stimulate the young
people through social skills.

We actively worked at the social skills session, seeing again and
again young people revealing many things about themselves.

We were challenging young people about their racist views,
employment, violence, work, politics, challenging young people to
communicate and look at others' views and perspectives.

We found that once one or two found employment then a
snowball effect happened and others followed suit. In an area which
has high employment and where jobs of the type we require are
scarce (labouring, semiskilled) it has been gratifying to be able to
place as many as we have done.[4]

. . .

Though jobs were found, it was difficult to lift others out
of total apathy. It was easy to accept the status quo, to accept

there was no work, to accept a life of boredom. The community programme expanded to eleven posts covering Mayflower receptionists (part time) minibus driver, Sports Hall assistant, maintenance man, as well as those working in the Day Space project. The greatest individual help that Day Space gave was to Hanson Raffo. He became the supervisor and wrote:

CP for me has made me proud, made me more willing to try things that I would not have tried before. It has given me so many experiences, i.e. writing reports, looking after money, working with people, being sensitive to people's needs, working with a different range of people, phoning people. CP for me has given me an insight into the future, and I will be more prepared to do something positive and not just any old job. [5]

· · ·

He was accepted for training by YMCA in September 1985. Doug left in May 1985. With the two gone, the Day Space team were finding it impossible to supervise the club building and make the programme happen. Day Space had become just a daytime Senior Club as far as the 'clients' were concerned, but with less than half the number of workers. There was damage to equipment and to the building and it was closed down.

Although the community programme continued to fund some of the other posts at Mayflower, there was increasing unease that the young people were being used for jobs that should be regarded as regular long-term ones. They were leaving after a year with no real prospect of a job to go to and because Mayflower was stretched, the training content was not great. It was decided not to renew the application. In any event yet another set of government schemes was coming in on a different basis. It meant a greater financial commitment on Mayflower's part where the job was essential, like receptionist but that was considered right.

In the early 1980s Alan Craig came and operated out on the street trying to reach young people with the gospel. During one summer break when the club was shut, a number of young people who had been linked with the club made Christian decisions and started to come to church. Alan worked with them doing Bible study in his kitchen. The group stayed together for quite a while and some of the youth team were drawn into working with them. Alan remembers.

I was in touch with them when they were just growing up and they received quite a frosty reception in church. The spiritual side soon died and never picked up. It's always been a tradition here – they get a burst and the church doesn't accept them. You need to set up a church for them to start off with – not long term. They want life and noise and chatter. Let them make their own church and then grow into the adult church. Kids like this don't have the self-control and discipline and quietness that older people do. Either you chase the older people out or you chase the young people out.

. . .

So there was very little obvious 'spiritual' fruit from the youth work for a number of years. However, you can never know what seeds have been sown. Periodically Pip Wilson would get a letter from an ex-member who had a genuine encounter with Jesus Christ and wanted to tell the only person who had talked about him and demonstrated him before. John Dove whose story is included came back after spending several years in clubs here.

As with all Mayflower activities it is impossible to do justice in a short chapter to all the work, the team weekends, the individual commitment, the joys and sorrows. In the end young people's preferences changed.

Rosemary Finch, heavily involved in Newham's borough

youth work reflects. 'The large numbers in youth clubs began to drift in the early '80s and go down dramatically. I think that's why the local authority in the end decided to close some clubs and actually put people into outreach work. In the '60s young people flooded to clubs, by the '80s they'd done it. The youth club members were getting younger and younger. By the time you got to fifteen you'd grown out of it. Therefore you were either there because you wanted to mess it up or you had other things to do.'

Patrick Butler
Learning the Hard Way

For a young Christian with a leaning towards youth work and a desire to share his faith, nothing could have been more exciting than the prospect of living and working at Mayflower. 'Youth work in the East End' had a glamorous ring to it and if I'm honest, the impression I got of a rough area with tough kids only served to increase my excitement and anticipation in coming here.

Thinking back to my first night in Senior Club, my expectations of the kids had been considerably off the mark. It was disturbing to encounter clean, immaculately dressed, tough teenagers when I had expected them to be scruffy, rough and untidy. Their toughness combined with self-confidence and a razor-sharp wit made me uneasy. They spotted a difference in me that meant I was easy meat – and they knew it!

For any 'outsider' coming into contact with the inner city, there is a learning process to be undergone, no matter how enthusiastic or well-meaning that person may be . . . it took me at least a year before I didn't feel 'new' in the club any more. I suppose I expected to be able to relate to the kids fairly quickly and that any differences in background would soon be overcome. It took a few incidents, however, before I realized that it wasn't going to be me who set the pace!

Patrick Butler

The most memorable lesson came early on and involved Fellman, Booze, Phil, Johnny and a few others chatting with me by the coffee bar. Booze pulled me aside and whispered, 'Ask Johnny how his mum dances.' I was reluctant, feeling very unsure of my ground, but not wanting to appear a spoilsport, his persistence soon won over my uncertainty and I asked Johnny how his mum danced. A deathly hush fell amongst the group and Johnny grabbed me and thrust me against the wall. I heard murmurs of 'The bastard', and 'fancy asking him that'. Johnny, with a fist held close to my face warned me colourfully and in no uncertain terms what would happen to me if I ever said anything like that again, and it was only when he let me go and I backed off shaken and confused that Booze explained that his mum was in a wheelchair and hadn't got any legs!

It was a classic 'wind-up', I know, and there were others – not as cruel perhaps, but still just as painful. Even so I am grateful for such incidents as they served to put me in my place early on . . .

The differences in values and attitudes I grew to realize were very deep-rooted. In a talk he gave at Greenbelt in 1981, Roger Sainsbury (ex-Mayflower warden) summed up some of the differences like this:

Those of us from middle-class backgrounds have different cultural attitudes and norms which we clothe ourselves in. In a changing society it is not easy to classify, but the following table may help.

Middle class	Working class
Individuality	Group loyalty
Judgmental	Accepting/kind
Privacy	Openness
Stiff upper lip	Vulnerability
Facts	Feelings
Meetings	Meeting

Another noticeable difference was my black-and-white attitude towards right and wrong. There seemed to be certain practices in Canning Town that were okay, such as fiddling any system or buying stolen goods, and others that were not okay, such as 'grassing' (informing). There wasn't necessarily any loyalty to the clear standards that I had been brought up with and held as universal.

My most illuminating conversation on the subject was with Fellman as we chatted in a pub one evening. He put it like this: 'I know that stealing is wrong and I know that you see it that way too. If black is black and white is white then I agree with you and where you come from this is probably the case. But when you come from round here it's different.'

When I came to Mayflower I had been a Christian for nearly two years. During that time I had challenged others and shared my faith in a way that had borne much fruit. The prospect of God using me in the same way at Mayflower excited me. But as the weeks wore on, it seemed increasingly difficult to talk about Jesus. Although I would get to know people better, there seemed little interest in the gospel and it was hard to find common ground on which to share it.

Where I had been used to dialogue and debate and people challenging my faith, often themselves searching for a meaning in life, here there was none. Some of the kids, it seemed, hardly thought beyond the here and now, let alone the eternal destiny of their souls! Sometimes there would be serious debate, but often this would only reinforce the commonplace negative attitude towards the gospel. As Phil put it: 'I just can't believe in something that isn't there. I'm not that sort of person.'

It became more frustrating however when I realized that it was often my background that was deterring people from seriously considering my message. Comments such as: 'It's easy for you to believe, nothing much has gone wrong in your life', or 'the only reason you believe in God is because you're a Christian,' seemed to imply that because of my background, I had no more choice about being a Christian than I had about the colour of my eyes!

The following excerpt from a conversation I had in late club also serves to make this point . . .

Phil asks me what I was like before I became a Christian. 'Well', I say, 'I used to be pretty self-centred and a bit dishonest at times.' This cracks them up laughing. Is that the best I can come up with? As on previous occasions the culture barrier is evident. I can see them write me off as just another bod who found it no problem to become a Christian because he didn't do anything wrong anyway.

In my early days, any conversation about Jesus meant a great deal. They seemed like real breakthroughs – oases in a dry hot desert. After one such conversation I wrote: 'It's one of those moments when you want to pray so hard because they're admitting so much. Opening themselves up much, much more than usual. You feel the door must be wide open for Jesus to walk right in and you don't want to let the moment pass.

Alas, these moments did pass and we never seemed to move on from there. Booze always wanted to talk to me about 'the Lord' though, and this excited me until I read in a 1976 youth-work report that Booze had been talking about the Lord in exactly the same way five years previously!

But I still had hope. In 1982 I wrote: 'It can be so hard to share the real Jesus with the kids and times like these when you really feel you've got something to build on count for a lot.' Again these feelings passed and it seemed that what was sown could never be reaped.

David Sheppard in a recent television lecture talked about something that I believe helps to explain the reluctance of inner-city people to accept the gospel. He called it the 'poverty that imprisons the Spirit'[6] and it suggests that a person's social environment will affect his likely response to the gospel. The poverty in Canning Town is not so much financial as emotional. Things happen in kids' lives that mean they have to shut off certain feelings and responses in order to survive. Hurt after hurt, disappointment after disappointment mean that kids develop a tough exterior. If nothing can penetrate, then nothing can hurt.

Sometimes 'Ten o'clock News' at the end of Senior Club will spark off an interest in the gospel and one or two members have become genuinely interested in becoming Christians, talking and sharing deeply what it would mean to give their lives to Jesus. But it always seems that peer pressure prevents it going any further. 'I would but it's me mates,' is a common statement. In Canning Town group loyalty is paramount. The risk of breaking away from the norm is too great. As one lad put it, 'Around here it's easy (meaning in Mayflower), but out there it's impossible.'

Gary, one of our older club members, wasn't doing much one Tuesday night so we both sat in the group room and watched the video of *The Cross and the Switchblade*. It was a powerful film and I prayed that it might have some impact on Gary. Two hours later we discussed what we had seen. Gary didn't deny the truth of the story but he said he couldn't see that it made much difference whether a person became a Christian or not. Then, with disturbing clarity he summed up the situation at Mayflower as he saw it.

'You might as well face it,' he said, 'Pip and you lot have been trying to make us Christians for years, but you try and name one person who's been converted. No one becomes a Christian round here.'

This time I didn't even have an answer. He had it in a nutshell and it hurt because I knew he was right. He wasn't trying to judge or ridicule, he was just stating a fact. But he had highlighted one of the most disquieting issues facing us: 'Where are the results' It is a painful question, no matter who asks it, as it implies failure and suggests that maybe you've been 'doing it wrong' all this time.

After having worked here for seven and a half years as senior youth worker Pip Wilson wrote: 'Seven and a half years and no one wants to know Jesus! That's how I was feeling that evening. Low, discouraged, loving Jesus, but very, very (pick your word!) pathetic.'[7] Now, after just three years I was beginning to feel some of the pain and frustration also. Stories like *The Cross and the Switchblade*, although encouraging, could also become depressing – Yes, God can miraculously change the most hardened lives – but why isn't he doing it here?

David Sheppard once wrote: 'A Christian youth worker must have an infinite capacity for disappointment.' I did not have this infinite capacity and I began to feel my faith lose its credibility. It became hard to pray or read my Bible, and to have any hope or faith became a struggle. In his book *Discipleship*, David Watson wrote: 'One of the greatest inspirations for a Christian is to see lives change.' Here there was no such inspiration and I could feel no power in my message.

One of my greatest struggles was in coming to terms with a thriving Christian scene away from the 'coal face' of the inner city. I became cynical of other Christians and their stories of spiritual success. 'Just try that here and see how far you get!' I would think to myself.

I still feel it is easy for people to judge the success of Christian youth work in terms of those converted and to see the role of the youth worker as an evangelist. There is more involved, however, and although all Christians are called to 'account for the hope you have within you', a game of snooker or football, a trip out or a chat about the latest fashion may be just as important in meeting the needs of the kids as, for example, a Ten o'clock News spot.

The aim of youth work, however, is to help kids to reach their full potential and get the best out of life, and as a Christian I believe that the very best can only be found in Jesus. Thus we should feel satisfied when sweaty bodies come out of the gym after a hard evening's football, but we should never see this as an end in itself.

There came a time when I had seen so little 'spiritual' activity either in my own life or elsewhere, that I began to question the whole concept of 'Conversion'. This came to a head in August '83 when I heard that a group of inter-club boys and girls had become Christians. Apparently it had happened through a Senior Club member who had been converted over the summer holidays and they were now all having Bible study in the chaplain's house most nights of the week. Somehow, I found that I couldn't rejoice in this news. It all seemed so unlikely. Surely this was just another wind-up – kids out for what they could get once again.

However, in September, Dave and I were given the task of leading them in a weekly discipleship group. This group has now been going for almost a year and although some have dropped out and others admit that they only said they were Christians for a laugh, there is nonetheless a group of eight or so who are involved in the church and still serious about being Christians.

Through working with the CSC group (as they are called) I have realized that there is a temptation to look at conversion in black-and-white terms. There have been great encouragements and great disappointments and sometimes I feel sure they are Christians, other times I think not yet.

When does a person become a Christian? Is it a definite line that you cross over – from darkness into light? Or is it a line that you may travel along for a while and at some point (you may not know when) you realize that you are now a Christian? Perhaps it is both.

When Jesus was taken off to be crucified, Peter felt totally dejected. The man in whom he had put his whole trust, who had loved him, performed miracles and healing had been exposed as a cheat and was to be killed. So where were the miracles now? Was this all it amounted to? You can imagine how Peter must have felt.

And yet the miracles had been real, Jesus's promises were true and all would be eventually made clear to Peter. But in the meantime he was on his own in the cold, stark reality of everyday life – no power and no miracles.

People love success stories. Although I have seen few 'successes' at Mayflower, this is certainly not a story of failure. I feel in many ways like Peter – having been made to question – seeing no miracles – waiting for all to become clear. I know that there were times when I wanted to 'come in from the cold' and to feel once again the 'inspiration that comes from seeing lives change' – to go somewhere where it all seems to work. I know many inner-city youth workers have reached that point at some stage. But Jesus never said it would be easy as one of his disciples. In fact he made it clear that it would not be. Nonetheless we all need times of refreshment to recharge the batteries and get that 'saltiness' back again. C.S. Lewis once wrote: 'Along the road the Lord refreshes us with many inns, but we should be mistaken if we were to think that they were our home.'

It would be easy to say, 'I have done my bit' and then retire to an 'inn' of my choosing, but as I go on to study youth work at Manchester, although I hope to receive the refreshment I need, I pray that it will only be that I may return to serve Jesus better in the future.

Whatever I have given at Mayflower, I know I have gained much, much more.

Coming in from the Cold
John Dove

I probably came to the Mayflower when I was around seven or eight in 1975. I don't come from a Christian background. The Mayflower was always used as a youth club, somewhere to go to get kids off the street. It's changed a lot over the years. It used to be quite a rough-and-tumble place with beat-up rooms and quiet rooms.

I was always boisterous when I was younger, up to about age ten or eleven. I was abused sexually and I went really into myself, really withdrawn. I couldn't tell my mum and dad about it – I felt it was my fault; I felt guilty and dirty. I never told anyone. Mum and dad knew there must be something wrong with me because they were saying, 'John you're not going out with other kids,' and 'it's not natural you keep locking yourself in your room; what's the matter?' I wouldn't tell them – not until thirteen years later as a Christian. So they used to lock me out onto the streets of a day. At the time I just felt like I needed my mum and dad the most, the security of their home, being there safe and to know that they loved me. To me, they wasn't there for me at the time when I needed them most. It was like a big rejection. I've always had good parents. They've always been quite strict, brought us up in a way that's good and proper. It was a miscommunication both ways which really brought us apart.

For comfort I used to come round to the Youth Club. I used to sit there on my own. I used to try and put on this tough exterior for the world that I was just one of the boys and I was all right, but inside I always felt inferior to everyone. I always felt different and insecure. I think Pip Wilson used to be the leader and Doug. They used to notice that there was something about me. They used to try and coax it out of me; 'Was there anything wrong at home? On the streets? Or at school?' They were good people, I knew they loved and cared for me. One time I broke down crying in front of them and they tried to tell me about Jesus and God. To me at the time it was like an imaginary friend of theirs who they'd got. I'd got real problems . . . if only you knew the pain and the hurt I've got inside, and you're trying to tell me about this imaginary friend of yours. You're mad. Going to the big school, instead of me being the bully, now I was being bullied. It was like rejection all round. Not only was I the black sheep of the family, I wasn't wanted in school. It was hard for me to make friends. Most kids when they grow up say they want to be rich or famous, want to be a policeman. I just want to be happy. I used to tell myself that one day I'm going to grow up and my mum and dad are going to love me, be proud of me and that's what kept me going.

When I left school I got in with a crowd of fellows who lived local

John Dove (right)

in the area who I'd grown up with. We all came together in a closer way 'coz we used to share the local boozer. They were all into drugs, these friends. Whereas I'd been bullied through school and rejected by everyone, they accepted me for what I was. I always believed the drugs was wrong. I could never have sex with a girlfriend as I was scared of sex because of what had happened to me. They used to taunt me about that but basically they accepted me. When I kept turning the drugs down they started to leave me out of the picture. I couldn't take any more rejections so in the end I started to take the drugs just to be accepted. I found as soon as I took the drugs it gave me the self-confidence I'd lost when I was a young teenager. It numbed the pain and hurt inside. Drugs quickly became a lifeline. I had quite a good job and all my money went on them. Mum and dad wanted to know where the money was going. I got moody indoors, more and more rows with my parents, got chucked out, forever coming and going. Each time I got back it seemed to get worse and worse. The more problems I was having the more drugs I was taking to forget about them. I was stealing to keep my own habit going, to supply myself.

Then I turned my attention towards the spiritual. I believe drugs open the spiritual doors to your mind. I became interested in the supernatural – UFOs, the occult, witchcraft, anything like that. I started to look for a purpose in life through those things. I used to go to fortune-tellers, tarot cards, astrology. It seemed like the more I delved into it the more certain I was of really why I was here. I always believed I was put on this earth for a purpose. The relationships got worse. The situation in my home got worse. I was taking more and more drugs to forget my problems. Over a period of years I was so bad that in the end my mum and dad didn't want anything to do with me. I lost my job, my family chucked me out, I lost my girlfriend. This all happened in about a week to two weeks. I was so depressed I just went out and took loads and loads of drugs and collapsed. I believe I nearly died. So my life was in such a state then that I cried out to God. There was nothing else to try. I said, 'God if you're there, come into my life and change me 'coz the way I'm going I'm destroying my life, everyone's life around me, and my life's going nowhere.'

After I said that prayer I was going to court and I had a few months where nothing seemed to be happening in my life. I seemed to be living for each day, always depressed. The probation officer got me a flat. I moved in and was decorating it up, putting furniture in and I forgot about the prayer to the Lord. I got a magazine through the door about Jesus – to me it was like a miracle. I remembered the prayer and it was like God moving in my life in a real way. It wasn't like someone in the area had just pushed a magazine through about Jesus; this one had come to my address from America. To me that just blew my mind. It was like God saying to me, 'I'm here and I am real! I read this booklet about Jesus and nothing made much sense. But I was interested, I wanted to find out more. One thing that really made sense to me was at the back it said if you went out and bought a washing machine you get the instruction book with it. So God left the instruction book called the Bible. I thought that really makes a lot of sense, so with my next giro I went out and bought myself a Bible. I stated to read God's instruction book.

It was over a period of a few months – I just started at Genesis and read through to the New Testament. I just knew that God was real. There is so much wisdom in the Bible, I knew it couldn't have come from man. I knew it must have been inspired by God. I knew I'd found the answer to life. When I was reading about God's laws and how He's holy and perfect and His plan for mankind, when I'd seen how much short I'd fallen of that, the things I'd done wrong in my life, I started feeling guilt. I tried to put the Bible down, not want to read it 'coz it was too challenging but I found I couldn't. Something made me just keep on picking it up. After reading through to the New Testament and reading how much God loved, Jesus Christ said 'Any man who comes I will never turn away. If he seeks he will find, if he knocks the door will be opened. If he asks it will be given to him.' I just knew it didn't matter about the drugs, about all the lives I'd destroyed around, the state my life had got in, I knew that God loved me for who I was and not for what I was. I knew then at that moment that I needed to give my life over to the Lord.

So the Mayflower was a natural choice for me to come to. The next week I went to Mayflower's evening service. I sat at the back and at the end of the service they asked if anyone wanted to come forward. I quickly ran out of the church. I went back a week later and Johnny Ringwood, one of the elders of the church, came up to me and took me to the front of the church and sat me down near the front. We talked about my life and at the end of the service he asked me if I wanted to ask Jesus into my life. I said 'Yes' and so I went forward and made the commitment.

Just before I became a Christian I read the Bible in the Old Testament and it said, 'Keep the way of the Lord and make your mum and dad proud of you.' I really kept that in my heart and it really spoke to me. The first thing Johnny Ringwood challenged me to do was go home and tell my mum and dad what I'd done.

I just went home and said 'Mum and Dad I've just become a

Christian and it's because I love you and am sorry for the life I've lived, sorry about all the hurt I've brought you.' Mum and dad started crying. It's amazing 'coz the first thing they said was, 'We're proud of you.'

My dad doesn't believe and my mum says she believes but she's not prepared to do anything about it. As time's gone on they've seen Christianity for me is not totally what they expected. I deny myself, I don't go the way of the world. I think they're quite challenged by that because it shows up the sin in their own lives. I think they accuse me of being overzealous and a bit of a religious fanatic at times. There's been a bit of friction over that in the past but they'd rather me like that than what I was.

First of all I tried to give up everything overnight. I tried to stop smoking, stop doing the drugs, drinking, stop fighting, stop telling lies, stop working and signing on, stop thieving. I just couldn't do it. I thought I could never be a Christian – it was just going to be too hard. Someone said to me that I can never change in my own strength. Otherwise we wouldn't need Jesus to die upon the Cross if we could reach God in our own strength. It was only Jesus and his Holy Spirit in us that could enable us to change. Just to let God do it in His own time.

Gradually my life just carried on as usual except that I was reading the Bible every day, praying to God to change me. I found that instead of striving to change but praying to God and asking Him to do it for me and through me, I found that I was changing. Something was happening inside without me being aware of it. Where I was always swearing, for example, I found when people swore in front of me I was becoming offended. If I accidentally swore I found myself immediately saying 'sorry'. Then I was compelled to tell the truth – even if it embarrassed me or put me at odds with someone. That's how I found the Spirit of God working in me. Just challenging me, one thing at a time.

I knew I didn't need the drugs – to me it was more the habit. It was me having to put my willpower into action. You could say doing it in your own strength but it's a two-way thing – the power of prayer and asking the Lord to give you the will. I found that first of all I stopped taking the pills and carried on smoking the pot, then I stopped smoking the pot, but I carried on smoking cigarettes. Then I was challenged to give them up. It was gradual.

After five months of becoming a Christian I was baptized.

I do feel the Mayflower is quite a special congregation. At the moment we're striving to go out on the street and preach the gospel to get people into the church. We want to see more people in the church, especially young men. One of the advantages of a small congregation is that everyone knows each other on an intimate level. It's like a big family – everyone's there to encourage one another, support one another. That's really good and that's really helped me in my Christian walk.

When Mayflower opened the Vincent Street hostel, Carol Forza who's overseeing the work, came up to me and said she believed God was telling her that I would be making an application to move into Vincent Street and that it was an answer to prayer. I said, 'No, Carol, I don't know what you're talking about, it's the furthest thing from my mind.' I just walked away.

Not long after I was due to go on holiday with my brothers and their friends and again people said to me they believed the Lord was really challenging me and as a Christian should I be going on this holiday with non-Christians, getting up to smoking and drugs, sex and drinking. I said 'No it's all right, I'm strong in the Lord.' Again just going off in my own power, believing that I was super spiritual and would battle against the forces of evil.

Instead of listening to what God was telling me through the other Christians, I went on holiday and I got trapped into that – not trapped, I had my own free will – but I believe that actually I came out of the will of God and was then open to the attack of the enemy. I quickly got involved in sex and drugs and drink. I actually took a real battering and found it so hard to come back after falling in such a big way.

One good thing that the Lord has given me is spiritual openness with my church leaders. I went and told them and instead of them being sympathetic which is what maybe I was hoping they would be – giving me a pat on the back and saying, never mind – they really took me to town and disciplined me. It made me really pull my socks up and sort my priorities out. I find that God doesn't take our problems away and He's always disciplining us, always chastising us, putting us in our place.

What I learnt I learnt the hard way early in my Christian life. I've tried to bring God into my plans instead of putting myself in God's plans. I think the Lord is bringing me to that place now where He's helping me to learn that God leads and I follow.

It's been hard for me to accept commitment. We live in an area where you're almost forced into a way of life, an area where if it feels good to do it, if it gets a bit hot round the collar and you find yourself in a situation you're not totally comfortable with, you can always opt out. In that sense people in Canning Town have no real backbone, no commitment. And I've grown up with that, not knowing any real discipline.

I found out when I became a Christian that it's not for weak people. It actually gives you strength. You have to be strong to stand up, to go against the tide of popular opinion and stand up and be different. I often view Christians as stallions who have been broken in. If you take a wild stallion and you break it, it hasn't lost any of its power, it's just controlled. That in itself has brought out a sense of self-worth in me and encouraged me. I can get up and speak about the Lord now whereas before I had no self-worth whatsoever. God's turned my strong points for His glory into His right perspective.

Losing Our Balance
and Finding it Again

(1982-1993)

WITH THE COMPLETION of the major redevelopment and the new staff team in place, Roger Sainsbury felt his task had been completed. There were long discussions within Mayflower and in the wider borough network as to who should replace him. In the end it was decided to appoint a warden who would have responsibility for the Centre and the staff team, and a chaplain who would have responsibility for the church. Edward Furness and Peter Watherston were duly appointed and were licensed together in January 1982.

Peter Watherston remembers:

It was a bewildering place to come to. The different parts of the work seemed to be fragmenting. There was a powerful staff team already in place. The youth work dominated the rest with three full-time senior staff members, residents and helpers and with its own management committee. The local church, though in theory at the centre of everything, appeared to be sidelined. There were local people involved in the youth work, but practically none were church members. The local church saw little, if any, visible results in terms of young people coming into the church from what appeared to be a big and expensive youth work. The youth team felt increasingly isolated. They were facing the violence of the local community and felt that the local church either had no idea what the culture was like or responded in fear, trotting out simplistic answers, like cracking

'Did you hear the one about . . .?' Peter Watherston (left) and Edward Furness (right)

down with rules, banning or closing clubs.

At a theological level, in the face of the lack of response to the Gospel, an urban theology had been developed in FYT which seemed to downplay the need for repentance and the validity of conversion. There was still a lot of tension between the 'incomers' and the locals. Although there was a lot of talk about empowering local people and an indigenous church, there appeared to be no local person in any significant position of leadership except Rich Gerard as community worker and a Pastoral Assistants' group in the church whose role was undefined.

What was the vision? How could we reconcile the different interests? Staff relations became strained. We spent time with bits of paper with 'Sports Hall', 'Youth Club', 'Nursery School' on them trying to fit them into a coherent jigsaw. Was there any alternative to splitting the church off from the rest of the Centre? Other questions crowded in. Was Mayflower's high public profile right? Were we trying to play on people's guilt by presenting Canning Town as a hard, deprived area? There *was* real deprivation, but were we presenting a dishonest picture of our spiritual success?

. . .

Roland Allen is not the only writer on mission and leadership, and under Roger Sainsbury's wardenship a different model of urban ministry was developed. But in wrestling with the relationship between incoming leaders and local people and between the bigger missionary institution and the newly planted Church the dilemmas that Allen struggled with in Africa at the turn of the century had close parallels with the struggles Mayflower has had in the East End of London. He writes:

The theory is that the Mission stands at first in a sort of paternal relationship side by side with the native organization; finally it ought to disappear and leave the native Christians as a fully organized church. But the Mission is not the church. It consists of a missionary, or a number of missionaries, and their paid helpers, supported by a foreign society. There is thus created a sort of dual organization. On the one hand there is the Mission with its organization; on the other is the body of native Christians, often with an organization of its own. The one is not indeed separate from the other, but in practice they are not identified. The natives speak of the 'Mission' as something which is not their own. The Mission represents a foreign power and natives who work under it are servants of a foreign government. It is an evangelistic society, and the natives tend to leave it to do the evangelistic work which properly belongs to them. It is a model, and the natives learn simply to imitate it. It is a wealthy body, and the natives tend to live upon it and expect it to supply all their needs. Finally, it becomes a rival, and the native Christians feel its presence as an annoyance and they envy its powers; it becomes an incubus and they groan under the weight of its domination. In the early stages it maintains a high standard of morality, and in all stages it ministers largely to the advancement of the native community by its educational and medical establishments; but it always keeps the native Christians in check and its relations with them are difficult and full of perils. [1]

Peter remembers going away after eight months with two friends for a week's fasting and prayer feeling totally inadequate and ill-equipped for the work, with no answers to the questions being raised. I had felt in the two months before coming to Mayflower that God had spoken very clearly about the building of a visible community of God's people living together in a new way, not in an isolated country retreat but in the midst of the East End with all its tensions and pressures. We seemed to be a million miles from that. I felt above all I needed a supernatural anointing of the Holy Spirit to do anything. There were no great flashing lights or fresh revelations that week — just the two words as I left 'Trust me.'

In October 1984 Pip Wilson wrote: 'For the first time I have thought that it is becoming impossible to run a club in Canning Town.' He described the aggressive and dangerous atmosphere involving knives and large fireworks. 'The kids are so aggressive and explosive that even I — twenty years a full-time youth worker, including ten years in Canning Town — cannot handle these hard, tough teenagers.'[2] There was no opportunity to make contact or build relationships. The team were simply trying to stop bad incidents and 'policing'.

Pip proposed stopping open club work with seniors, doing detached work on the streets, attempting to start group work and intensifying the depth of the work. This was followed by an even more devastating evening when five regular members started to smash the club up and riot. The police were called.

Pip and Doug left the following May. They had both given ten years to the work and needed relief from the accumulated effects of the battering they had had. Paul Vincent and Colin Primett were appointed. Senior Club was reopened for periods but closed again. The police were now more frequently called. Colin only stayed four months. In his final report he wrote, 'The job had more pressure than I had the experience to handle.'

The senior worker's post was readvertised but no application was received for a period of eighteen months. Rana Johal, a converted Sikh who had trained at the London Bible College, joined Paul Vincent. Attempts were made to start activity-based groups but these had limited success. In the spring of 1987, it was finally decided to stop all senior-age work and Paul left in April.

Rana, who was then the only youth leader, wanted to focus the youth work again on bringing the gospel to local kids in a style appreciated by them. He began a weekly youth worship using the New Hunt launderette. It was well-received and a number of the young people made an initial commitment to Christ. Barbara Graham was one of those and is still very much involved in the fellowship and particularly in the music on Sundays. Again a good start was made, but difficulties arose with how far to keep them as a separate group and how far to integrate them with the adult church. Rana left in June 1989 with the issues unresolved. With his departure virtually all open youth work ended and no replacement youth leader was appointed. What had started as a youth work project thirty years previously, with the aim of reaching the young people of the area for Christ and with the hope that youngsters would come through the club into the church and become future church leaders, had threatened to overwhelm all the rest of the work and had itself been destroyed.

Before the final closure of the open youth work, Peter Watherston remembers:

We had struggled over setting down the vision for the future and staff members swapped drafts. Summer 1985 seemed to be a turning point. Three of the senior staff left, we bought the Huntingdon Arms pub and the vision paper flowed off the pen almost ready-made and was accepted. There is a bigger vision than building an indigenous church – it is 'proclaiming and living out the kingdom of God.' That vision is common to all churches. There was a desire to spell out what it meant as clearly as possible. Some will disagree with certain emphases. Some external Mayflower Council members questioned the unqualified way we spoke of sharing what we possessed with one another. But having set it out, how should we take such a vision forward?

Later that year I read Tony Higton's book *That the World May Believe*, setting out the way Hawkwell Parish Church had set out to implement a very similar vision. Here was a very practical model to work from. My wife, Hannah, and I attended a leadership week at Hawkwell and a team from there came to a weekend at Mayflower where we shared with the congregation and the Mayflower Council the vision for the Centre. The Hawkwell team spoke and demonstrated the way God had led them.

The initial work was to strengthen the church, restoring its life and structure as far as possible on biblical principles – putting it back as the hub of the Centre. This involved developing our corporate prayer life, learning to 'hear' God through prophecy, pictures and the gift of tongues for the direction He wanted us to pursue. It involved releasing our worship so that we could enter into joyful praise and make use of the gifts of the Spirit. It included working for the church to become more united, 'one heart and mind' as the New Testament puts it, as we show a deep love for and sharing with one another committed to a common vision. In particular this meant breaking down the barriers between incomers and locals. It meant restructuring the church and Centre so that we were less like a hierarchical institution and more like a functioning body. It involved establishing a pastoral leadership and church discipline which was authoritative but not overdominant or legalistic. It meant working for justice in all our dealings including, because we are an employer, wages, employment and voluntary work. It included a renewal of our desire to reach out evangelistically to our area to see people won for Christ and brought into the fellowship and to reach out in practical care so that we love our neighbours as ourselves.

...

These things are not achieved overnight nor without argument, hassle and strain. If you move in these ways, particularly in the gifts of the Spirit, there will always be a feeling by some of there being first- and second-class Christians — those with a hot line to God who saw pictures or spoke in tongues and those who did not.

As this new direction was being set, two new projects were being developed. Both aimed to reach out to the local community but not with a separate work run by a trained professional nor dependent on external funding for running costs. As far as possible they were to arise out of the life and witness of the church.

In 1986 the external Mayflower Council agreed that the management of the recently purchased Hunt pub should be in the hands of the local Chapel committee. A survey was organized of local opinion as to its use with a hundred and thirty questionnaires being completed as people knocked on neighbours' doors in the area. The overwhelming request was for a launderette with café facilities for light refreshments. The committee hoped that the upper floors would accommodate young Christian workers who might oversee its running. It represented a natural meeting point and was an obvious place for outreach and evangelism. No paid worker was taken on to run the launderette. Within a year it was wholly run by local people. This was a big commitment needing two people a session for ten weekly sessions of four hours each. The leader of each session was to be a church member, but the helper need not be. The New Hunt was self-financing in that the revenue from the machines and the coffee bar paid for the £600 a month rental of the machines and the other overheads. It soon became a very good drop-in meeting point and a place which would draw people from the local community untouched by the other work of the Centre.

There was also a desire to pick up employment and training again in the face of continued high unemployment. With some disillusionment with government schemes, it was decided to try to establish training and work experience in a real, commercially competitive environment without relying on changeable government finance. The aim was to share skills, to develop people's confidence and abilities in a sheltered workshop setting and to encourage and support them as they moved into the next stage of their development. Hannah Watherston who had run her own dressmaking business in Yorkshire became the Garment Workshop supervisor.

Hannah set up basic sewing and pattern-cutting courses lasting twelve weeks. Those who wished stayed on for production experience. This meant the need to develop and market a range of products. It was decided to specialize in children's clothes. Initially in 1988 no one was paid, but

Mind your fingers – Liz Stanley in the garment workshop 1989

after fifteen months it became possible to start paying wages. The aim was for those working to share in decision-making and for everyone to receive the same hourly rate of pay. This was before the introduction of the principle for Mayflower as a whole. A further aim was to be self-financing. A grant was received for the purchase of machinery and an interest-free loan for stock. Sales were very difficult until a young Christian designer, Pauline Mullaniff, joined the team. Orders were obtained through children's fairs and shops. With a lot of hard work, turnover was pushed up from £5,500 in 1989/90 to over £25,000 in 1990/91 and the workshop just broke even without any grant aid.

On the church side a commitment course was introduced, loosely based on one developed by the Hawkwell parish taking out overwordiness and adding in other issues such as social justice. All church members were encouraged to attend to lay a firm foundation together in Bible teaching on commitment to Jesus, to the local body of Christ and to the world around. At the same time there was work on the structures. There had always been the feeling that the local people could take responsibility only for the local church and a few other matters, but why couldn't they manage the whole complex? Did Mayflower have to be fragmented to make the best use of it? The buildings fitted together as a single unit.

Over a two-year period there was a careful movement towards the point where the overall management could be passed over to the locally elected church council. Mark Birchall, who served Mayflower for thirty-five years, including nine as external chair of the Mayflower Council, wrote at the time:

Over the two-year period the 'outside' members of council met to discuss our hesitations, often deeply felt, about the timing of the changes and method. I spent time with members of the Chapel committee and others from the local church, and heard all their doubts and fears as well. We talked it all through at Council meetings and hammered out a draft 'how it will work' document; we explored the changes necessary to our Memorandum and Articles of Association. We rejoice that in the end our decision was unanimous.[3]

• • •

Who should be the church members — those responsible for electing the new local council? Peter Watherston writes:

We believed we needed a strong, committed group and introduced an annual service for people to renew their commitment to the vision and work. One of the problems of electoral rolls is that they become out of date in terms of current involvement and we are not a parish church.

We wanted to establish common biblical goals for our Christian lives, not to create legalistic hurdles for people, but to challenge us to lead the transformed lives set out in the Gospels – We will all fail in our Christian behaviour and round here that failure can be extremely public and messy; where there is genuine repentance there can be forgiveness and a welcome back seventy times seven times, however painful that hurt has been; where there is no repentance we only insult the person by pretending the thing hasn't or isn't happening or that it doesn't matter – If we were to be effective we needed a group who were committed to those goals together and just as we renew weekly at Communion together our experience of confession, forgiveness and new life, so annually we would reconfirm those goals together. We hoped that as we grew, more people would come into the commitment. Those that didn't were still very welcome at all the services and activities of the Centre but would not elect or serve on the Mayflower Council or attend the weekly growth groups. The idea was to have a growing united group at the heart of the work whilst remaining open to our local community.

This caused some resentment, particularly among some older members and those who were no longer regular worshippers. Jim Gosling, who by this time was ordained as a non-stipendiary minister, firstly based at St Luke's and then being extensively used in the Newham Deanery covering for interregnums and clergy holidays writes with Janet: 'Our eventual break from Mayflower was brought about by the policy of commitment. It is to our mind a particular failing when confirmed members of long standing are told that commitment made in the past by way of confirmation is no longer valid. For whatever reason we found this policy impossible to come to terms with.' The policy has remained controversial among those looking in on it. No one left the Church because of it but a number who had drifted away previously felt it made it more difficult to come back. A number of people have questioned how 'Anglican' it is. 'I cannot conform to Mayflower's non conformity' was one comment. There has remained an underlying unease that the policy is exclusive and too inward looking.

Grace Raggett, church member and cook here for thirty years, found it difficult initially. 'I always considered myself committed to God. When we had to go through the commitment course I did not see that there was any incentive for that at all. It did make me quite angry. I had heard of other churches that had gone through the same kind of thing and each and every one of them had failed. That was not encouraging. But when I did the commitment course I really enjoyed it. Although it was very basic, I just felt it was a renewal of listening to the Word, and we can never have too much of that.'

Another area of restructuring was in the staff. From the earliest days there was a distinction between the senior staff who would meet weekly for a prolonged period and the remaining staff consisting of cleaners, cooks, maintenance staff, bookkeeper. Part of the job of the senior staff was seen to be pastoral. This meant individuals were discussed and that carried with it the need for confidentiality. This could be quite threatening for local people.

The senior staff was also clearly the engine room of the Centre. Day-to-day running, sorting out problems and difficulties, thrashing out future policy and direction, holding the whole together — all this happened at the staff meeting. Mayflower Council was there as a sounding board and could take the decisions where there were conflicting views and help things through during major staff changes, but the basic decisions about use of buildings and activities were made by staff. The setting up of the local chapel committee meant decisions relating specifically to the church were taken there, but the staff meeting remained the dominant decision-making body for the Centre as a whole.

Another factor was finance. As senior staff were increasingly funded by the diocese, local authority, Department of Education for the nursery school or Urban Aid, nationally negotiated scales of pay were paid. Although these were not extravagant they placed the staff members on significantly higher rates of pay than other staff. For most of Mayflower's history money has been tight and local staff members have accepted a low rate of pay in order to make ends meet. There was also, because of the need to encourage incoming staff to commit themselves fairly long term and to guard against burnout, a policy of longer annual holidays for senior staff, coupled with a regular long leave every few years. Undoubtedly all these were beneficial for those staff members, but they combined to perpetuate a distinction between those coming in and those who were local.

For some time there had been a feeling that a move away from grant dependency would be positive. The borough went through a difficult time financially in the mid 1980s, not fixing a rate sometimes till after the beginning of a financial year and being rate-capped. Commitments to funding posts were ad hoc sometimes, almost quarter by quarter which meant a lot of insecurity for some staff. Mayflower wanted to appoint to posts local people who were not qualified and therefore were not necessarily recognized for grant aid. Mayflower also wanted to be more overtly evangelistic in its outreach at a time when multifaith and equal-opportunities issues were playing a bigger part in borough thinking.

Rana had written in December 1987, 'I believe we must not let anything get in the way of our presenting individuals with Jesus. Our first love as Christians is Jesus. As we go on, the gospel will become more overt. I know that some people will disagree with this, but in all honesty anything less than clearly presenting Christ to the kids we are responsible for is a dereliction of our duty and constitutes a failure to meet the stated objectives of the Mayflower youth work. We are Christians first — anything else — youth work, wardenship, community work is secondary.'[4]

Rosemary Finch, who by then worked in the borough Education Department commented,

In the 1970s I think you could have gone for the Gospel more than you can now. Things have changed with the multifaith issue. When Rana actually said he'd much rather be a Christian youth worker than an ordinary worker, in a report that was going to members and officials, other youth workers were extremely annoyed. Some of them were very political and said this shouldn't be allowed.

• • •

By the end of 1987 the youth work and Sports Hall grants had ended. There was left one substantial grant for the community work covering wages and overheads.

As part of the changing vision, a questionnaire was drawn

up about the role of staff meetings, the introduction of monitoring groups and pay and holiday structures. This was circulated to staff and local congregation. As a result of this, the Chapel committee decided it would like to move towards an equal pay, equal holiday position. This involved giving fairly substantial increases in pay to the non-senior staff. No one was to take a cut in pay, but as people left and new people were taken on, Mayflower would work towards a single hourly rate of pay. This coincided with the rundown of external funding and with the two-year period working towards the handover from the external Mayflower Council to the locally elected council. By April 1990, the full equal-pay policy could be introduced with the two remaining externally funded posts voluntarily covenanting back to the Mayflower the amount necessary to bring equality in pay. At the same time extra perks, free rent, expenses etc. were abolished. The rate of pay is not high (currently £4.50 per hour). This may have the effect of discouraging some people from coming, but it does affirm the value of every job being done at Mayflower and gives a bond of unity.

The introduction of the monitoring group system also reduced the importance of the staff meeting. Initially, the groups were very much building-based — Sports Hall group, Cooper Street group, New Hunt, youth club groups — but as the work was integrated the groups became more functionally based. The membership (about six in each group) is mainly drawn from Mayflower church members. No one is on more than one group and each group tries to have at least one and often two Christians who are external to Mayflower with the aim of helping it not to become too ingrown. Staff attended their own monitoring group meetings. The task of the groups is to pray for and support the staff, to act as a sounding board for new ideas, to draw up job descriptions and interview new staff and to agree the policy and direction for their area of work.

With the development of these groups the senior staff meeting was phased out. The groups meet every two to three months and take much of the detailed work of the local Mayflower Council which can concentrate on major decisions and initiatives and the growth of church life through the commitment courses, growth groups, evangelism, worship and intercession. But major decisions and initiatives have to come to Mayflower Council from the groups.

The decision to move to a local staff and an equal-pay policy inevitably involved a reduction in the wider involvement of Mayflower. David Berry, who was the community worker from 1984 to 1988, had built up a good reputation among workers in the statutory and voluntary sector in Newham. He was instrumental in forming and helping the coordination of a number of tenants' associations in the area. He became vice chair of Age Concern and played a significant part in NVAC and the Docklands Forum as well as the Labour Party. His contacts with the borough council kept Mayflower's name to the fore in community affairs. Dave was also instrumental in encouraging a local mum, Betty Tyson, to take on the position of assistant community worker. Although Dave reported to the monitoring group, the nature of his work meant he operated largely on his own though being a member of the church with Pip, his wife.

When he moved on and the post was advertised on the new equal-pay rate geared largely for a local person, Gordon Barley was appointed. Gordon's background on leaving school at fourteen with no qualifications, his involvement with the Moonies and drugs and his conversion is the subject of another book to be published next year. Gordon's approach to the job would be radically different from Dave's. He was to see it much more in terms of people. He got involved in Victim Support, the Newham Hospital Chaplaincy and individual visiting as well as the Advice Desk. As a result Mayflower's profile was reduced as the fairly high-profile youth leaders had also not been replaced. This has reduced Mayflower's influence within Newham and tended to isolate it in relation to other community groups. On the other hand, Gordon himself was enabled to develop within the job to the point where he has been recommended for training for ordination subject to doing two years on the Aston scheme to help him acclimatize to study.

The final element in the restructuring was the formation of the leadership team in January 1990. With the desire to establish Mayflower as a church on biblical principles rather than an institution, there was to be a leadership which was not based on staff position or function but on spiritual maturity and qualities of leadership. Edward's executive role as warden had been phased out with the new staff and monitoring-group structure and the titles Warden and Chaplain were dropped. Janet Gosling took charge of all central administrative work for the smooth running of the Centre. Edward and Peter wanted prayer to establish the right foundation for the new shape of leadership. Three members of the church were asked to pray, meet with each other and then individually with Edward and Peter. The Lord spoke clearly through that time about ministries and relationship together. It was felt that Peter should take the overall lead in the new team. In practice there has been no pulling of rank in what is a genuine shared leadership.

The congregation was asked to put forward other names for the leadership team. Peter and Edward prayed and chose Johnny Ringwood and Doreen Turner to make a team of four. Doreen was not at that stage a member of staff, but joined it later as part of the Sanctuary work. Johnny was a borough safety officer, vice chair of the local NALGO

Union and very involved in the local community. The team met for one and a quarter hours each week and twice a year took a day away together. It cannot take any executive decisions which means that any new initiatives have to be fully discussed by Mayflower Council. After three years it was decided to formalize the arrangements into an eldership and the original four became elders on Easter Day 1993.

How far could Mayflower be self-propagating, self-supporting and self-governing? With the structural changes the first and third of these were just about in place. The second will always be more difficult. Mayflower's social activities would stretch the resources of a 500 to 1,000-member church in an affluent area let alone a small congregation in an inner-city area. It continues to receive very generous financial support from a number of charities and trusts including Jerusalem, Smith's Charities, Goldsmiths, Beatrice Laing, CPAS, Hedley as well as gifts and covenants from many individuals and some churches. It is always very encouraging to know that people value the work sufficiently to give towards it and the warmth of letters of support and generous giving is tremendous. The award of the 1993 U.K. Templeton prize of £3,000 was also a very special recognition.

A number of fairly large centres have been built in Newham and elsewhere in the last few years. A common experience is that the biggest headache is not the raising of money for the original building but funding its continued use. Unless the originating body has very substantial reserves to continue funding, the Centre is always struggling. It usually decides to go for government or local authority funding which involves increasing form filling, bureaucracy and strings attached, with the constant threat that funding will be cut or legislation changed. Such funding will increasingly only be available for clearly secular work and the Christian content will be muted. The alternative is to try to generate money from the use of its facilities. This requires considerable administrative backup and the building is in danger of becoming simply a place which provides a space for a series of unconnected activities without having any clear identity of its own. It isn't a place of welcome for anyone coming in with a number of different staff members able to meet the needs of the caller, a buzz of activity and a warm atmosphere.

Mayflower has never fully used all its buildings. As it moved from having a large, professional funded staff responsible to an external Mayflower Council to a local largely unqualified non-funded staff run by local people, the emphasis changed with less use of the youth club and more of the launderette and workshops. Other groups have increasingly made their home there including Arklight working with young offenders, three African-based Christian organizations, the Peggy O'Farrell Dance School, Alcoholics Anonymous, Neighbourhood Care Project, a home helps group and a slimming school.

Numerous local clubs use the sports hall and the youth club each week and many organizations book the main Wallace Hall or the lounge for meetings or parties. It is good to see the facilities being used. However, it has been important for the place to retain an identity, to be a place for the Kingdom of God with a unity of purpose and organization dedicated to Him as a light in the community and not simply a set of facilities.

Over the years from the founding of the Malvern Mission there has been a desire for Canning Town people to take some responsibility for the financing. The first missioner wrote that if capital cost were met from outside, he thought they could generate the money for their own running costs. Kennedy Cox always argued that facilities and goods should not be provided free. People should make a contribution to what they receive. David Sheppard wanted local people to take responsibility for the chapel and when the local committee was established, a separate chapel account was run and charged with expenses relating to the running of the church. The accounts have now been consolidated together but as part of the annual commitment for the last seven years the importance of tithing has been emphasized giving a tenth of income to the church and Centre. It is a poor area; apart from those working at Mayflower (who are also asked to tithe) only two or three have full-time jobs and possibly a further four, a part-time job. The money generated is small in comparison with the costs. The principle is good but the place will always be seen in some ways as 'rich' whether the money has come from society balls at the Dorchester, government or local authority funding or charitable trusts. The tendency to perpetuate dependency is great and there have been a number of people who stayed while they were receiving 'goodies' and moved on when they stopped.

Part of the future vision is to see Mayflower turned round from being a receiving place to being a giving one. In financial terms, this would involve the East End sending money, goods, or skills to those in greater physical need. Firstly that means using its own facilities where possible to generate money for its own needs. This has been happening and a total of over £100,000 a year is being generated from activities and facilities. Secondly it means getting involved with overseas work. In November 1993, two Mayflower church members went with other Christians from a Baptist church in East Ham to Rumania. It is hoped this will be the first of a number of visits and there are discussions about the taking on of specific projects in conjunction with local churches there. Finally there is prayer for that spiritual breakthrough which would bring many into the church swelling the financial ability to help others.

Have the changes worked? How do people feel about

them? The next chapter reflects on the different aspects of empowering people, but some general comments are added here on some of the changes.

Carol Forza, a local Christian converted in 1989 says:

'People say that this church is for the people and Mayflower really practises that, because they actually let the people run it. They make the decisions. It's a way of life at the Mayflower, it's a community and we all take part in running that through being on the Council and monitoring groups.'

• • •

Mary Middleton, who has been at Mayflower for thirty years says:

'Right now we are a local group, people are local Christians that are all running Mayflower Centre. This is something of the vision that David Sheppard had when he first came here. It must be running it all right 'coz the Mayflower's still running! When it was run by outside people, with just a few Mayflower people on it, most of them were money people. They talked in millions and thousands. They used to get right above me and I used to go to bed and say to myself, "whatever were they talking about?". I just couldn't understand, but nowadays they do the financing a lot clearer and you can understand it.'

• • •

Grace Raggett says:

'Mayflower wasn't as one. It was separate parts. When Edward and Peter came they brought it together as one. It hasn't been easy and there has been a lot of people that have been hurt. But looking at it all round I should say that it's greatly improved. There have been forgiveness and repentance of the different people that have been involved here that went away very angry. But thank God for that, I think most of that has been resolved now.'

There has been a real breaking down of the artificial barriers. Sue Furness, Edward's wife says:

'When I first came here there was a them and us feeling, that we were "them" people from outside and everybody else in Canning Town was "us". They thought of us as very different. I feel that now in 1993 in the church that we stand equal before God as one body. God's gifts to each of us are gifts through His Spirit that he wants to give us and it doesn't matter whether we're people that have always lived in Canning Town. We're one body and church together before Him.'

A Personal Journey
Edward Furness (1982–1994)

'Take your hands out of your pockets. Stop looking like a headmaster. Come and meet everyone.'

'Get off your bums. It's time to dance.'

Memories of a welcoming disco in January 1982, as Peter Watherston and I started at the Mayflower, chaplain and warden respectively.

What a change from just six months previously, sitting in a small church in the New Forest. My wife Sue and I had heard the call of the Lord to leave Lambeth, after ten years as headmaster and physiotherapist.

'You did not choose me; I chose you and appointed you to go and bear much fruit, the kind of fruit that endures.' John 15:15. Words of Jesus brought to us in a small church in the New Forest just four days before the searching interview with the Mayflower Council and which were to come again to us just two days after being offered the warden's job, this time at a conference in London.

So at the age of forty, I arrived on a snowy wintry day, my elderly wheelchair-using mother, Sue, who is blind – and me! Preparing my first sermon, a brick came through the window – not exactly gift-wrapped with the message Welcome to Canning Town, but it didn't help our adjustment. Neither did the kids who later persistently nicked the heads off our daffodils or who tried to test out Sue's blindness by calling 'Mind the (non-existent) step' as she learned the routes to the Rathbone Market through the subway.

We missed enormously the multiracial community in South London, coming as we did into a totally white church at Mayflower, reflecting the users of the Centre, the staff and the local community at that time.

The life of the Centre and congregation soon became very special to Sue and to me right from the Licensing Service in a packed chapel (after which I calmly showed the Mayor of Newham into a cupboard instead of the kitchen!). The ease with which five hundred people were given cups of tea afterwards, and refreshments, was a sample of the hard work so many people put into the Mayflower, and still do.

My mum found it more difficult to settle, and the Wednesday Mums' group became her special place of comfort, though she continued to worship regularly, despite increasing frailty. Her faith in the Lord was strong, and she challenged her new friend Bridget Druce to come to church too – and she did as well as faithfully visiting her each week at home until my mum died in December after less than a year here. The funeral service in the chapel was perhaps for us a special time of bonding with Canning Town where 'your mum' means so much.

Sue and I had no children and we shared with the congregation our beliefs that the Lord would give us a family, seeking prayer and the laying on of hands as we had in our church at St Stephen's, Lambeth. We felt the lack of a buggy and one or two kids made us the odd one out in an area where extended families are the norm. In the end, we called a halt to seeking medical intervention because of the emotional stress and physical pressures this entailed: this did not seem the Lord's way forward, at least for us. Our prayers were answered in another way. In August 1985 we fostered Peter, with us from the age of eleven for five years, and the church shared our joys and hard times in many ways – not always with sympathy.

Looking back, though, this time enriched our following ministry to others facing a similar challenge of teenage pressures at home and school.

People often ask us where we go for respite – do we have a cottage in the country or a caravan by the sea? The answer is that we do not have either. Apart from the normal four weeks' holiday, we use the support of our local fellowship for strength and encouragement. Yes, this makes us reveal our own vulnerability, but it also enables others often out of their own weaknesss to minister the Lord Jesus to us. We know what it is like to have a boy excluded from school, for example, and how hard it is for him to maintain any self-belief, to keep any sense of purpose.

So I began to explore the warden role, aware of the prestige of the job in the borough and the wider church. I had to be myself, hopefully open to change, but with the skills and experience of twenty years in teaching and the last four as an ordained non-stipendiary minister. And fairly early on, I found there was a challenge to my understanding of the warden role, not from the local church committee nor from the Mayflower Council, but from some of the senior staff team.

Each week, the three youth leaders, the community worker, the nursery school head, the Sports Hall manager, the vicar of the parish church (St Luke's), the chaplain, the warden and all available wives met as senior staff. Most of us were highly paid compared with other staff, due to grant aid from the Borough of Newham and relevant professional scales. 'Why should you take the chair?' 'What do you know about local streetwise kids and evangelism?' The youth team questions came thick and fast and I rapidly felt deskilled and put down. My past experience was in no way affirmed, and perhaps more importantly, my theological standpoint seemed under threat. My starting point was that Jesus died on the cross for our sins, that all who came in repentance and faith to invite Jesus into their lives can know forgiveness, new life in the risen Jesus and know the power of His Spirit in their hearts. Did this not work in Canning Town? Did the good news that Jesus loved people as they are – did

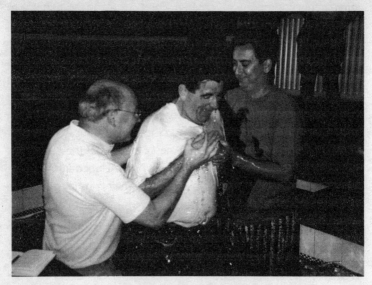

David Reid baptized 1993 by Edward Furness and Gordon Barley
at Custom House Baptist Church

this suffice? Was it too heavy to speak of the burden of sin to people
who were often put down and made to feel inadequate? Should I
look for conversions, for lives changed by Jesus, or was I to stay
alongside the hurting people for ever? And what about the Holy
Spirit about whom there seemed to be a respectful silence?

I realize now that for my part I failed to affirm the deep commitment
of the whole youth team to their task, the stress of working alongside
the local kids and accepting the abuse, the violence, the disregard
of the gospel. Pip Wilson has written vividly about this in his book
Gutter Feelings. This book tells some of the story too.

Youth Management committee meetings became for me a
particular time of pressure as we debated and made decisions about
the right way forward. The work was heavily subsidized by
donations in addition to the grants from the borough; workers were
often very stressed and drained by the face-to-face aggression of
many kinds; there were no signs of young people showing any

interest in becoming Christians and the local Mayflower congregation felt very detached from it all. As I argued for changes, I felt particularly out on a limb and remembered a promise from the Scriptures which became very special to me in those months. 'To those who were to receive what He promised. God wanted to make it very clear that we would never change his purpose: so he added his vow to his promise . . . So we who have found safety with him are greatly encouraged to hold firmly to the hope placed before us. We have this hope as an anchor to our lives.' Hebrews 6:17-19. How I needed that safe place! Tempted at times to look back and consider a return to the world of education, and also to think of a move to parochial ministry, it was the clear call of God to be here, and my desire to see His promise of 'fruit that will abide' which held me here. The Lord's promises are proved true in the pressure moments of our lives.

Sincere efforts were made by many people to help the staff team here to find a united way forward. Michael Eastman, Jim Punton, Mark Birchall are only some of those who agonized with us, but it was only as youth staff moved on from here that things began to change. New appointments were made, both to youth work and the Sports Hall, and three of these were black people – Rana Johal, Paul Vincent and Linda St Louis which was a significant step in the face of the racism of the local community, reflected inevitably in the Mayflower institution as well to some extent. The new emphasis on evangelism and the greater involvement of the local church caused us difficulties with funding from the Borough of Newham, and by 1989 all grant aid ceased. We needed time to reflect on what should happen next, and as youth staff and residents left they were not replaced. By 1990, the youth club building was in darkness, virtually unused, and the Borough of Newham was enquiring about leasing it from us for five years, though this never happened; the darkness never finally puts out the light.

The decision as to what to do next was for the local church to make through the Mayflower Council. As the youth work declined over ten years, so a major change had taken place in the management structures of the Centre. I was appointed in 1982 by a Mayflower Council which was mainly made up of people from outside Canning Town. These were men and women who were deeply committed to the Mayflower often over many years and several had been involved in a hands-on way in the early years. The Council also had some members nominated by the local church committee, but meetings were in the main dominated by those from outside and their dialogue with me as warden. Part of my vision was to reach a point where the local Mayflower congregation became mature enough to stand on its own feet, to make the decisions about the direction of the whole work here, and the use of resources. For too many years, I believed, there had been an unhealthy and unnecessary dependency on outside – often professional – skills and resources, and it seemed right to start to reverse this process to correct the balance. Not that it will ever be right to be totally independent, but the partnership with the wider Christian network would be on a more equal basis, with Mayflower giving as well as receiving. Nor was this just a financial vision – in fact that will probably be the last thing to happen, if ever it does. I thought more of a discovery of skills and spiritual gifts and ministries, a sharing of experiences and testimony, with the emergence of genuine local leadership.

My first meeting of the chapel committee showed the care I needed to take in sharing this vision. As warden, I was the chair, so I indicated my desire to allow others to take the chair in future. After a brief silence, Jim Levett pointed out very clearly that whatever I thought, this would be unconstitutional. He quoted the paragraph involved off by heart! So I chaired for the next year, but submitted a constitutional amendment to the next AGM which was passed. Rich Gerard and Steve Boulton in following years then showed great wisdom, humour and skill in leading this committee forward.

Steve Boulton probably made the greatest impact on me of all the East End Christians whom I came to love and respect. In his sixties when I came, he was almost a father figure with a deep wisdom and a heart able to understand the pressures of our changing church and of my role in it. He was always here – or so it seemed – whether when he was handyman full time or retired! Everything which needed repair, including me, was handled with humour and a wide range of gifts. Steve loved the Mayflower, and he loved Jesus. He was a walking talking history book of life in the docks, where he was a stevedore, and life at Malvern Mission and Mayflower. He started in the cubs here in the 1930s, and ended up as District Commissioner Boulton, MBE. His death in 1988 was a great loss of a man who so busily and wholeheartedly lived out his faith in Jesus among us all.

So in October 1989, after months of prayerful preparation, the local church elected the first local Mayflower Council, with Johnny Ringwood - local Cockney Christian - as its chair. For the first time, our own people were responsible under God for the Mayflower. Of course there were feelings of doubt and uncertainty, there would never be a time when the Centre was on an even keel for a handover of this nature. But people had prayed and believed the Lord was saying this was the time. Nothing which has happened since makes me believe we were wrong, though things have not been easy.

But back to 1989; already by this time there were signs of growth within the congregational life and in the work of the Centre, in people's lives. The development of a launderette and coffee bar on site in the Victorian pub we purchased in 1986 to complete ownership of the whole island complex of buildings was firmly in the hands of local volunteers under the leadership of Grace Raggett. She had been cook for very many years for the residents and now that they had left, this was a new outlet for her great energy and large heart. Grace had herself found her Christian faith had come alive in the Holy Spirit and the Lord led her to the work in the New Hunt (our name for the old Huntingdon Arms) with a vision to make it a place of welcome and outreach. In its first seven years, this project has proved a place of service and evangelism for many church members. There is a continued fight against gossip, moments when the takings have been short and when the team has lost heart, and Grace herself is no longer working there. But the Lord has sustained and kept this unique project which continues to touch the lives of many of our immediate neighbours - not only for their washing and drying – but also for this caring friendly welcome that has pointed some at least towards discovering Jesus. The New Hunt is also an example of the Lord's timing! For years – back to Dockland Settlement and Malvern Mission days – people have wondered when the pub building would be integrated into the work here. Charringtons closed the pub in 1985 and it went to auction. Despite a bid of £47,000, it was withdrawn and put up for a second time. During all this time we hadn't felt a freedom under God to make an offer. Then Philip Byam-Cook of the Hedley Foundation visited and saw the situation. He rang me the day before the auction. Through his contact with the Chairman of Bass Charrington the pub was ours for £37,000 and he offered the first £10,000 – but an answer was required by 4.00 p.m. After a hasty but imploring prayer, we accepted. By the time of completion of the sale, enough donations were received to cover not only the cost of purchase but also something towards the refurbishment as a launderette. How much we need to learn that when our will is in accord with the Lord's will we need not worry about the provision of resources. He provides when we are faithfully serving Him.

There were other signs too of local Christians taking on responsibility. Johnny Ringwood was chairing the Council and the attendance was almost always 100 per cent, Pat Lynch was in charge of the Sports Hall, Betty Tyson was learning new skills to run the Advice Desk and be the community worker alongside Dave Berry who had come from outside after Rich Gerard moved to be social worker at Newham General Hospital. Rich had been a stevedore in the docks before facing redundancy, and had worked at Mayflower in the 1980s to gain professional qualification to undertake the community work post. He was a lovely warm Christian man who brought to the work his own unique blend of compassion, humour and concern. Janet Gosling became office administrator for two and a half years working alongside Glad Blacker who does the bookkeeping (over twenty years at a time of writing) and is an invaluable link between past and present. Rita Auer continued to cook for the Lunch Club, consistently serving forty meals a day for the past nineteen years. Joyce Mealand took increased responsibility as housekeeper, and Hannah Watherston trained many local mums to gain new skills in the Garment Workshop. Bert Hughes drove the minibus for Lunch Club. Terry Mann was one of the new group who became Christians, and he became caretaker when faced with redundancy by Tower Hamlets. Doreen Turner opened the residential work in the flat above the launderette (more of this later) and Jan Shorter, Rose Griffiths and Chris Timothy continued reliably and carefully to do their work as cleaners. The Lord was using local people to take the work here forward, though many found this a pressure and a struggle and withdrew for a while to recharge.

But this was the visible side of the work. More importantly I think the Lord was doing secret work in the life of the small congregation (at times down to twenty or thirty regular worshippers). We were discovering together the promises of God in the Scriptures to renew and equip His people, through the life and power of the Holy Spirit. Peter Watherston believes 'the Lord has given Mayflower congregation a particular vision: to be a place of healing and sanctuary, where the good news of the gospel is lived out incarnationally by His people, and where new life can begin for all who will meet Jesus here and go with him.'

The community work, Advice Desk, Lunch Club and New Hunt all offer opportunities to be not only a servant church but to bring healing and the message of salvation in Jesus to many people. The facilities of the Centre are available for community groups to hire for leisure purposes and social activities. This is not only good for Mayflower financially, but well over a thousand people come through the doors each week giving opportunities for friendship and evangelism. Good stewardship of resources can challenge us to consider our underused premises, but we have learned not to be overstretched. Unless good leadership is available, activities are not a positive and can often have a negative effect. When the Lord opens up a door, His timing is right, and we need the ability to discern this and the obedience and faith to go with Him. 'Follow me' so easily becomes our running ahead of Jesus.

In the almost twelve years I have been in Canning Town, there has been a great shift of emphasis on how the life of Mayflower is projected to the wider world. We no longer major on the urban deprivation in which the place is set, nor the powerlessness and poverty of many people here: both are still true, and we do not seek to present a false picture of things. But local people are fed up with hearing that Canning Town is a rotten place, and that they need outside professionals to come and sort it out for them: that's not possible anyway. Such presentation, of course, attracts sympathy, prayer and very particularly money. All grant forms ask about 'the special needs of the area' and we do qualify for support in all sorts of ways. The Newham Needs Campaign is very vocal at the moment in seeking extra government funding for the borough.

But recent years have focused on change where local people are empowered to be the church, to take responsibility for all decisions and policies, even when they go wrong. I have encouraged people here to have a go at taking the lead whether in worship, in the launderette or whatever aspect of the place the Lord indicates: to look for the day when Mayflower gives as well as receives. So we gladly take groups to meetings or to lead services in other churches or organizations: so we have begun to tithe the chapel income and the rentals from letting out buildings (not donations since these are given specifically for work here). Peter too has urged us to look beyond Canning Town to our relationship with other Newham Christians, to begin to play a wider part in the mission of local churches, again on a two-way basis. As I write, preliminary talks are being held about the possibilityy of Mayflower taking on parochial status which would give a wider role for the church to play within the Church of England. Whatever the outcome, it is a sign of new vision, and I pray this will mean the seal on my ministry here receiving from the Lord 'fruit that endures'.

Throughout my time at Mayflower, God has given me a colleague with a common calling and vision. Peter Watherston was licensed with me on 17th January 1982, and our roles here were so intertwined that frequently people confused me with Peter, or Peter

The docks lie idle.

with me. We have prayed together, talked endlessly together, exchanged the wildest ideas in trying to discern God's will and agonized over the pain together when things have not worked out. The development in the recent years of a formal leadership team, and lately of an eldership with mature local Christians joining us, has spread the load of our responsibility under God for our ministry here. But Peter and I have had very special unity and purpose, especially in the early years, for which I thank God.

Empowering People

(1982–1993)

JESUS IN AN INCREDIBLY risky move turned to his motley group of disciples and said 'As the Father has sent me so I send you.' Who had they got to show them what to do and how to do it? He breathed on them and said 'Receive the Holy Spirit' and later he told them to go in his authority to all people, baptizing, teaching and making them Jesus's disciples. When they carried out this task the Jewish leaders were amazed to see how bold they were and to learn that they were ordinary men of no education.

Ordinary people plus the Holy Spirit can make a powerful impact. Empowering people has been at the heart of Mayflower throughout its history. Perhaps there has been more focus on this in the latest phase of Mayflower life. The characteristics of Canning Town have already been outlined. It is considered to be at the bottom of the list in Newham and Newham is near the bottom of the list in the country. All the pressures are not to take responsibility, to accept or moan about decisions taken for you. No wonder there was a policy to try to protect potential local leaders from outside influences which would draw them away. But despite that policy those potential leaders have moved away — some not far, to East Ham and Plaistow, but they have left Mayflower for varying reasons.

Moving is part of a whole change of life style with a change of job, monthly pay, mortgage, new goals and hopes. That can alter people's views of the area and the people they have moved away from.

Rosemary Finch commented about Bill Turner. 'The biggest thing it seemed to me was when he came out of college he felt he was an intellectual. He used to spend hours, 'til one or two in the morning talking with residents because he felt that they would give him intellectual stimulation. Therefore there was a great gap between him and Doreen who would be left on her own.'

Jim Gosling speaking of his NSM course at Oak Hill recognized the problems many working-class people have in getting into courses. 'The robustly self-reliant few who through dogged determination gain such places have to change beyond recognition in order to do so. In consequence they lose much of their original distinctive flavour.'

Will Mayflower always find that those who successfully are empowered by it will move on physically or emotionally? Will those who stay be those who don't want responsibility, are terrified by it and duck out of it? Not necessarily. The changes of the last few years have taken it back to basics. Hannah Watherston said, 'I think the biggest positive is that basically we're a lot of broken people — and we don't need to be afraid to be broken'

There is an enormous excitement in finding Jesus in the midst of brokenness. Carol Forza who had been through one marriage with a husband who beat her up and spent time in prison was on the run from him, had overdosed and gone to hospital. 'I was drinking from half ten in the morning — bottles of sherry, anything really that I could afford because it numbed me. I didn't feel that I wanted to face up to the past, to what was happening now. I thought if this is life I might as well just top myself and have done with it because it's holding nothing for me.' She was introduced to Toddler's Time at the Sports Hall run by Pat

Lynch, another local mum. After a while Pat suggested Carol came to the church. Carol says, 'I made a commitment to the Lord three years ago and I still had a drink problem. Things gradually got better. Just weaned myself off it really. Filled my life with other things — God. It's given me a sense of purpose. I'm needed. Got self-worth — a job to do in life and an aim.'

Chris Timothy described vividly the effect of anorexia. How she abused her body because she was terrified of being fat and her husband walking out on her. 'I call it Satan's disease because you deceive people when you've got it; you lie, you cheat. I wore bulky clothes to make me seem heavier.' Chris had ridden on her bicycle past the open-air evangelism that Mayflower does at Rathbone Market and used to stop. 'The moment someone used to come over to talk to me I would speed off again.' One day at home Chris reached a crisis point. Something or somebody told her to look in the mirror. After wrestling with herself for a long time she did and was horrified by what she saw. In her panic she screamed 'Jesus, help me.' Immediately she seemed to calm down. There was the sudden realization that Jesus was there. Both Carol and Chris are convinced that if it hadn't been for Jesus they would both be dead.

That experience doesn't end with conversion. Chris Timothy says, 'The way God speaks to me is I'm praying about something when suddenly the solution comes just like that and I think why didn't I think of that? Then I realize it's God telling me, giving me that idea. Sometimes I don't want to do something "Oh what's the point" and I still do it and then I realize I'm glad I did that. It's God giving me a kick up the backside. Go on Chris move it.'

Chris went through the agony of her husband leaving her for another woman soon after she became a Christian. 'I did pray to the Lord that he would do something about my marriage. I was thinking, Andy would go all night fishing as he often did and the Lord would appear to him. I really believed that. I got more and more disappointed. More and more praying "Lord do something", but when it broke up I thought Lord, what are you playing at? You can't be serious. You don't like marriage breakups, you're not going to allow this to happen. But then something told me God doesn't like murder but he allows it. God doesn't like robbers but he allows them. When I realized it was over for good it was as if the Lord was saying, 'Well, don't worry, hold on to me.'

Sometimes there have been worries about imposing middle-class 'quiet times' on Canning Town people. As the Bible comes alive God will do the prodding. Chris remembers, 'It was the Book of Job, and I don't know why I prayed and then suddenly said "Job". No verse, no chapter, just the Book of Job. So, it was this guy loving God and the Devil said, "Well, if you did this he wouldn't love you." And I found that a comfort. I thought Satan is having a go. I got up the next morning and thought, right. I just got Andy's belongings, put them in a duvet cover. And when he came round he couldn't get his key in the lock 'coz 'I'd had the locks changed. I said, "There's your gear, would you take it." I realized then I didn't need him. I knew it was over and there was no point fighting for something that was dead. I opened the Bible to read it and came upon a page where it said, "If you are married to a non-Christian partner and they wish to go, you must let them. I thought, Ooh, Ooh, I've been trying to bring him back.'

People have sometimes agonized about finding an authentic way for people to pray here — a Canning Town way of praying. Experience has been that if people want to pray they will do so. Pat Lynch was aware of the prayer support she had when her daughter Rachel ran away for three weeks and her son Martin was getting in trouble with the 'Old Bill'.

'**It was prayer** support that brought me through that. As I went to Growth Groups my prayer life has really strengthened. The biggest change in my life is the realization of how much the Lord uses me in prayer, especially in praying for healing for other people – physical, mental. I've had so much prayer answered.'

. . .

What came to be understood was that you don't have to be a vicar or even clever for God to communicate with you and use you. Hannah Watherston remembers coming as a resident. Her background had been in a Pentecostal church near Doncaster.

'**We were told** as residents that the gifts of the spirit and the baptism of the spirit was fine but it wasn't right for the church. If we had those experiences they needed to be kept private. Speaking of the time that the church was beginning to explore the gifts she says, 'For me the dynamic of prayer had begun to be released in my life and particularly the gifts of the spirit other than speaking in tongues and interpretation. We began to see that actually God wanted to communicate with His people and not only through His word, the Bible, but also through the gifts of the spirit. And so we began to search out and exercise much more the gifts that were prophetic and words of knowledge, and that opened a whole new dimension that I'd never been introduced to and for me that was good.'

. . .

Sue Furness also remembers that time:

'**I do often hear** from the Lord a picture or sometimes a word of knowledge, or in different ways, whatever the Lord chooses. I learnt how to do this from what I was taught in the Mayflower Church. Of course he talks through the Bible as well. We've got to hold everything in the balance. I think the Word of God is the most important thing that you can hear. Sometimes the Lord can give

Last orders please – Grace Raggett in the Launderette

verses as well and that has happened to me. When the Lord actually gives you a word to speak out, that is a very strange, scary experience. You might sit with your heart thumping, feel yourself getting hotter and hotter, thinking is this really from the Lord, should I really say it? And yet when you do say it, somehow you get other words that come into your mind and they are not from you, they're from the Lord.'

...

Grace Raggett says,

'I have pictures, words, words of knowledge – I have had pictures which were painful to share but I go to the person because as we know the Lord does give specific names at times and I have thought that it's best to share them in private. Which I have done and certain people said that had been quite true.'

...

There has been a recognition that every Christian can receive particular gifts or ministries and one of the tasks of the Growth Groups has been to discover what these are for one another. This is partly by observation but also through prayer in 'hearing' God for one another.

Betty Tyson looks back a few years to the time her gifts were discerned. Each member of the group contributed something.

'When they brought these things they said I'd be working with children and someone said I'd be praying for people not just people in the church. At the time I said, "Well I don't think you're talking about me! It must have been somebody else! Working with kids, oh sugar!"'

...

Now Betty is leading the club work with juniors and taking them away for weekends and is involved in one-to-one talking with people from her Advice Desk and visiting contacts.

It was increasingly being seen that God by his Holy Spirit could not only intervene and guide but could also deal with the past. At one level the past has been dealt with at the Cross. There is a tendency in Christians to bury bad experiences and to pretend that all is well with their lives. If they can't keep the pretence up they will drift away from the Church with a sense of failure. Everyone has had painful experiences where they have felt rejected, abandoned or let down. Often the reaction to that has been resentment or bitterness which can surface violently in anger or fear when triggered off by a new set of circumstances. The sense of being broken people is particularly strong in Canning Town.

With the development of the gifts of the Spirit came the discovery of prayer counselling. Through the Hawkwell link the method developed by 'Wholeness though Christ' was introduced. Hannah and Peter were counselled over three days by the team at Hawkwell and three or four went on their schools. Chris Timothy put it clearly, 'Prayer counselling is really basically to get to the root of your problem through prayer. Not being nosey but to weed things out. Anorexia, no matter what walk of life you come from is based on rejection. And it was the Spirit of Rejection that was in me and just would not go. And it had to be literally driven out by Peter. Sounds funny, but it did go in the end. It tries to come back but I know what it is, I recognize it as soon as it tries to come, and I'm not having none of it! And now, I weigh four stone heavier than I was then and I'm normal size.'

Having introduced prayer counselling at Mayflower, a number of people took advantage of it. After two years a training course was run to bring more local people in to do the prayer counselling. Doreen Turner took over responsibility for it. No one is under an obligation to have it but the majority of church members have chosen to do so.

Being able to know God's healing and deliverance was adopted for the church as a whole not just for each individual. In 1987 a weekly meeting for intercession was set up. Its aim was to 'hear' God and pray through areas of Mayflower work. Over a period of weeks and months it was felt God was pointing to the youth work.

As the group looked back there seemed to be a particular hold that had always prevented that work fulfilling its potential. At the very moment when real spiritual and developmental progress was being made there was unleashed a violent force which destroyed the work. This had not happened once but on a number of occasions and each time had succeeded in destroying what had been built up. In addition, looking back over the people who had led the youth work, many of them had suffered severe depression or breakdown, marriages were broken, finances sometimes wrecked. Burnout has been talked about frequently in inner city contexts, but this seemed to be different from burnout. As prayer continued, a number of different areas were identified but didn't seem the answer until the words, 'death and destruction' kept recurring.

Peter Watherston remembers going away from the prayer meeting thinking, 'If there are spirits which have held this place, where did they come from?'

Quite casually Peter picked up a book with a chapter describing the early Mayflower years and there in a single brief sentence was a reference to the fact that the Dockland Settlement buildings had been used as an emergency mortuary during the devastating destruction in the area during the war. On enquiring where this was located, it was discovered it was in the buildings which were pulled down to make room for the new youth club buildings

A while later, soon after the youth work closed in 1989, a group went into the club to pray. As they did so one of our fellowship, Barbara, a local mum, was clearly in distress. Deliverance was prayed for the building in line with the guidance received. Afterwards Barbara said that she had an intense experience like a very fast newsreel going on round her with many people flashing before her — a mother holding up a dead baby, others groping round searching in rubble, people crying. In the end she saw a hideous unhuman figure hovering overhead and as deliverance was commanded and the group prayed in tongues it swept downstairs and out through the front entrance.

Many will think this fanciful, grotesque or auto-suggestion. It in no way takes away the responsibility to work through prayerfully the issues involved, but it was felt to be one part of the problem which couldn't be ignored.

Seeking God's specific direction has also happened in the more formal decision making. This had the effect of making decisions more corporate, taken by the church as a whole. Grace Raggett and Janet Gosling describe what happened at a meeting to discuss the future use of the top two floors of the Cooper Street building.

In March of this year (1988) the Cooper Street Monitoring Group held one of their 'usual' meetings, but there was nothing usual about the outcome of the meeting. In fact, the meeting turned out to be an incredible prayerful experience for all those who took part.

As we prayed, various verses and words were shared. Matthew 9:13. At the end of the call of Matthew the tax collector. 'But go and learn what this means: I desire mercy not sacrifice. For I have not come to call the righteous, but sinners.' Although we are all sinners the most obvious sinners were those who had been in prison. We prayed about how we need to be caring and not judgmental – desiring mercy not sacrifice. During the discussion afterwards there was common amazement at the strength and unexpectedness of the Lord's leading. Further times of prayer brought forward the idea of a sanctuary.[1]

* * *

In July 1989 the local Chapel committee, about to take full responsibility as the new Mayflower Council, held a meeting at which six of the borough council's officers presented the case for the borough taking a five-year lease on the youth club building for community education activities. At a time of tight finances and when youth work was at a low ebb, taking one building off our hands and receiving a £10,000 annual rent for its use was attractive. Johnny Ringwood, the chair, proposed the committee adjourn for one week during which to pray and think. On reconvening there was virtually no further discussion. Each person felt individually they had 'heard' from the Lord including those most in favour of the proposal. The decision to turn down the offer was unanimous and taken in half an hour.

One further example of this corporate hearing from God and involvement was the timing and method of developing the Cooper Street building. In 1982 it was felt that another major appeal could not be launched so soon after the £1 million redevelopment. Could Mayflower follow the pattern of Nehemiah in handling it themselves under God, making no appeals for money, trying to do as much of the work themselves and waiting on the Lord for his guidance at every stage of the work, stopping and starting as He thought fit? Rich Gerard wrote: 'Obviously there are doubters of the method we have adopted, but overwhelmingly there is the feeling of excitement by many members of the church.'

It proved very difficult to operate on this basis of stepping out in faith. One builder went bankrupt and another committed suicide. Apart from one resident who did some carpentry work, it proved impossible to do the work from home-grown resources. The work stopped and started several times. But from the time of the new vision for the building's use in 1988 there was a real expectation. There was considerable concern about taking on a £250,000 contract with only £30,000 in the kitty and Johnny Ringwood in particular felt the pressure of this. Again as the meeting started with praise and worship, there was a peace and a unanimous conviction that the timing was right.

It did not always go right. At this same meeting it was also decided to take on a retail shop in Shepherds Bush as part of the workshop project. Shortly afterwards after prayer and discussion it was also felt right to appoint a supervisor to start the new woodwork workshop. Both these initiatives proved in the end to be abortive, painful and expensive. Mayflower was on a steep learning curve in praying, discussing and decision making.

Hannah reflected on the workshop experience: 'There have been failures but I think there have been successes as well. The successes are that a number of people were given training that would enable them. Liz could get a job in cutting if the situation was favourable, Marion is continuing sewing. Zelma could get a job in sewing if she wanted to. Vicky is setting up her own business in children's clothes. In terms of business as with a lot of businesses in the recession, it failed. So there are lessons to learn. I don't think it's ended. I think the workshops are going to be a very big part of the work in future years.'

Were local people capable of taking on the management of the whole complex? The first major challenge occurred within three months of taking over full responsibility and came from the borough council.

The conflict touched on several important issues — whether to take a stand on a particular biblical principle; the whole issue of partnership with a local authority and the conflicting loyalties it can produce; whether to accept withdrawal of grant aid or fight it as an issue of social justice; involvement with other churches locally and acting in unity together.

It arose out of the decision to turn down the borough's offer for the youth club building. One of the reasons for this was that Mayflower's trust deed required the promotion of Christianity. It was felt that the borough's use of the building might conflict with that.

The council's officers picked up this issue, stating that a condition of grant aid was that a group was totally able to accept its equal opportunities statement. (Mayflower had in fact produced its own statement two years previously which had never been challenged.)

Edward Furness takes up the story.

Johnny Ringwood and I were called to a meeting. There we were asked about the openness of our policy for allowing groups to use the Centre. For example, would a group of Muslim parents be allowed to teach the Koran here to their children? Or a group of lesbians to promote their life style here? We answered 'No' to both questions on the grounds that both the worship of other gods and the practice of lesbianism are contrary to the Scriptures. Both situations were totally hypothetical.

The Bishop of Barking, the Rt Revd Jim Roxburgh, was consulted by the local authority officers. He was particularly concerned about other borough-funded church projects. He wrote to them to point out that the Mayflower was an independent trust, and that 'views expressed are not necessarily official Anglican statements.' He sent a draft policy statement on the issue from the London Churches Group, and indicated that in his view there was no essential incompatibility between the local authority equal opportunity policy and the Christian faith. Mayflower was sent a copy of this letter by the local authority in support of their stance.

Matters moved quickly, but not yet publicly. In January 1990 the authority's local sub-committee agreed that Mayflower's activities be monitored for six months with a view to the withdrawal of grants, then at £25,000 a year, for community work and playscheme. The sub-committee also recommended that council members should not attend meetings at the Mayflower, and it should not be used for council meetings. This effectively isolated the work here from the community we serve as groups were immediately afraid to identify with us for fear of loss of funding or because they needed councillors to come to their meetings. Our rent income was considerably reduced.

This proposal raised many issues. Were voluntary groups not able to put boundaries on who used their premises? Were all groups to be asked such specific questions? No actual breach of equal opportunities in the delivery of services had been proven. We were being judged by what might happen. Finally the proposed reduction of grant might well limit the resources available to Mayflower, one of the largest providers of service to the south Canning Town community, identified frequently as the most needy area in the borough.

So in January Mayflower Council agreed to lobby the Social Services committee meeting the next month and request speaking rights. We invited Newham Christian Fellowship to join us in strength at the next meeting as observers and to lobby councillors with us meanwhile. The response was amazing, and well over a hundred people turned up to pray and listen to speeches from Johnny Ringwood and myself and the committee's response. The room at East Ham town hall was packed, the usual barracking and shouting of protesting groups replaced by a silent, prayerful crowd, packing the space around the councillors as they sat at their tables. Our case was presented and heard with dignity, but other committees also had to consider the issue before decisions were made and little was conceded at this stage.

John Oliver took a helpful initiative in organizing a meeting at Mayflower with a number of Christians who were active as local councillors and in the Labour Party. The comment was made that Mayflower's record on race issues and equal opportunity was beyond reproach. Had it been wise to answer the council officer's questions about teaching their faith to Muslim students and promoting a lesbian life style? After all they were only hypothetical. Mayflower leaders felt it had been right to make their position clear even though the situation had not arisen in practice.

Two other developments occurred of great importance. Firstly the whole dispute became public just before the meeting when the local press picked up the story from an inaugural meeting of a Newham Gay and Lesbian Rights group. The radio/TV media also promoted the story, views were expressed publicly by Mayflower and by councillors and the positions seemed to polarize. Misreporting and the involvement of extremists made the outcome seem inevitable. We did, however, receive scores of letters of support, and a few of criticism and were aware of the importance of not coming to a 'fudged' outcome. Our position was valid: activities at the Mayflower were open to all individuals of whatever faith or none and whatever their life style. But we could not allow our premises to be used for the propagation of other faiths or of homosexual practices which are contrary to the biblical position. The Mayflower was widely known as a Christian project and our boundaries come from our understanding of the Scripture.

Secondly, the Bishop of Barking wrote again offering to chair mediatory talks. He appealed to both sides to draw back from damaging confrontation. He recognized the valuable cooperation enjoyed over many years between the council and the Mayflower. 'The Mayflower', he wrote, 'has worked with public funding and with its trust deed. The council has worked with the voluntary sector and within its equal opportunities policy; let both continue to respect each other.'

So later in February, six councillors and four Mayflower Council members met with the bishop and his urban officer, in the council chambers at the town hall. After long, honest discussion of the dispute, the groups edged towards agreement. The bishop pointed out that all groups – even the borough – had boundaries on their lettings policies. The current dispute hinged on whether the borough's equal opportunities policy was prepared to heed the consciences of people of the borough in certain areas of its application and on whether Mayflower could agree the principles of equal opportunities in a policy of its own, maintaining its Christian integrity.

Mayflower Council subsequently agreed the following policy statement in March 1990:

'The Mayflower Family Centre affirms the principle of equal opportunities, in the belief that all people are equally creatures of God, with equal rights and responsibilities. We recognize that Newham is a society diverse in race, culture, creeds and interest and that no person should suffer discrimination on the basis of race, gender, disability, age or sexual orientation. Mayflower will seek to practise equality in serving the community from its distinctive position as a Christian organization. The Mayflower's activities and facilities are equally open to all within the boundary set by the law and the teaching of the Bible as traditionally understood. In the recruitment of staff, the Mayflower will have regard within the same boundaries only to the matter of experience, suitability and qualifications for the proper discharge of appropriate duties. Staff appointed will normally be practising Christians.'

This was submitted to the council and eventually accepted. The grant was paid in full for the community work, though many local groups continued to be cautious of using the Centre and relationships with some councillors are still strained.

One year later, our application for a renewal of the grant was turned down, not on the grounds of equal opportunities but because the council wished to find new areas and types of community activity for which we did not qualify!

· · ·

The locally run committee had had a fiery baptism but had come through a little bloodied but unbowed. In the July 1991 *Mayflower News*, Peter Watherston wrote:

So after many years of support our last borough grant has gone. Undoubtedly we have benefited from that link and we have very much appreciated the borough's concern and help. But in recent years there has been an increasingly narrow focus on work eligible for grant aid and an increasingly strong control from the local council in what is done and how it is done. There is a real danger that voluntary organizations receiving grant aid will become puppets of the authority. Though we face an uncertain future we value having the freedom to move in the way we believe God is directing and *to trust Him for the resources needed to get there.*

. . .

In practice there has been no reduction in any of the services Mayflower provides and the healing and sanctuary hostel has been added to the work. In each year the accounts have shown a small surplus despite the loss of local authority grant aid. The Lord has provided in other ways and Mayflower has not been the loser.

But the takeover of full responsibility has not been without its strains. The system has creaked. Initially the monitoring groups involved a few people in a lot of extra meetings. Some groups have flourished more than others. There is a difficulty for the external members of the groups in knowing quite what their role is and feeling there is a 'Mayflower Policy' which can make them feel excluded. Local people have found it difficult to take on the chairing of these groups and to feel any confidence in the managing role of staff that the groups have. Preparing agendas and writing minutes do not come easily. This has meant that oversight and decision making has not been efficient. These issues are still being wrestled with. In many ways it is easier to bring in a professional manager/administrator to pull things together. But would that be right? Has Mayflower tried to move too quickly away from reliance on professional staff? Is there a need to train people to fit into an efficient supervisory role or should there be an acceptance that discussions and decisions will be taken rather differently.

One way that has encouraged growth and maturity in local Christians is for the difficult, the ugly and the messy to be shared wherever possible.

The appointment of the supervisor of the woodwork workshop was an example of this. With the approval of Mayflower Council one of the monitoring groups interviewed and made the appointment. The family moved from Scotland into one of the Shaftesbury houses on the Mayflower site — Peter and Hannah moving in with Edward and Sue for five months to make way for them.

There was such a clash between the new supervisor and Hannah which in the end led to his refusing to attend meetings with Peter as chair of the monitoring group or with any other group at Mayflower. The monitoring group had a number of difficult meetings trying to work through the best course of action with people walking out at times. The leadership team was regularly involved with trying to bring about a reconciliation. The local Mayflower Council had the task in the end of terminating the staff member's contract only three months after his appointment. Meanwhile, the church was praying for the right outcome to the problems. It was a very painful experience and yet it was a growth point. Everyone had to accept responsibility for decisions already taken, to work through intractable problems, to pray together — to wonder what God was saying. The easiest way out was to resign or walk out altogether. No one did that.

During the Billy Graham mission in 1989 a Leyton man, Jimmy, who had been friendly with two local families for some time gave his life to the Lord, was baptized and went through the commitment course to become a committed church member. He was arrested by the police on a charge of sexual abuse after he took swimming the children of the families he had been close to. There was an immediate outcry and Mayflower had to decide what its response to Jimmy should be. He was denying the accusations and wanted to remain part of the fellowship. On the other hand a petition was organized locally to demand that he should not come onto Mayflower premises. There were wild rumours and much gossip. From the beginning it was decided to be as open as possible with the church about

what had happened and what decisions the leadership team
and the Mayflower Council had taken. This helped greatly
to defuse the situation. Jimmy who had previous
convictions was found guilty nearly a year later. Again it
was a very painful experience.

Joy Ryan who had known Jimmy for sixteen years felt
betrayed.

'I'd brought him to church and helped him to become a Christian.
I felt as if he'd stabbed me in the back – and it hurt. I think the way
I worked through it was really by letting all the anger come out. By
praying. Everyone in the church knew what I was going through.
They were praying for me and I was able to sit and cry in church.
I felt more close to the Lord in church as well . . . people used to come
and put their arms around me or their hands on my shoulder and
say, "we know what you're going through, Joy. But we're here for
you. Don't keep blaming yourself all the time – it's not your fault." '

●●●

Jimmy was introduced to a Baptist church in Leyton which
he is still attending. There is still good contact with the
children of one of the families involved.

The sharing of difficulties has its dangers. It can be
abused. Tensions have arisen over the development of the
healing and sanctuary work. On the one hand, the way it
was set up with Edward, Sue and Doreen sharing a home
with the other residents is informal and encourages sharing.
There is the desire that the church should be involved in
befriending and supporting. But there is also the issue of
confidentiality. Carol Forza commented 'The workers in
Cooper Street were so frightened of anything getting out
that they couldn't share. It was like a closed shop. There was
some bad feeling through misunderstanding. I think more
people from the church are now becoming involved in
Cooper Street. They are not feeling so insecure now and

worried about what's going to happen.'

There is a natural curiosity in some people which can cause real problems. One of the high points has been when residents in the sanctuary feel able to speak in the church of the reasons for their being at Mayflower. No pressure is put on them to do this and a number never do. Two in particular stand out.

Anne was in the sanctuary for eighteen months. She found it too difficult to stand and speak and so recorded her story on tape for the church to listen to. Her story is one of continual sexual abuse from the age of five, her introduction to a witches' coven with all its rituals and drugs, her rape and abortion at thirteen. She found some real release through the ministry of the sanctuary and came to the point of sharing that.

She did not know that Sean, one of the other residents at Cooper Street, had served some years in prison for sexually abusing children. When Sean was able to share his story in church in August, Anne had a sharp reaction. But the following day they were able to sit down together and talk things through without anger or guilt. Both had found healing through Jesus and could recognize the other as a brother and sister in Christ.

The sharing of these experiences has been a growth point in the church. The occult and sexual abuse cause a lot of fear amongst people. There needs to be great care in the handling of each issue and each person, but being able to face these things head on and to know there are answers and new life in Jesus is a great encouragement.

Soon after the opening of 5 Cooper Street an article in the *Newham Recorder* began, 'Murderers, sex offenders and robbers will find a warm welcome at Mayflower Family Centre.' The article was positive towards the work but inevitably sent alarm bells ringing amongst the local community. A petition was started to close the hostel down.

It was to be sent to the Archbishop of Canterbury and the local member of parliament. It soon had several hundred signatures. Mayflower's response was to invite anyone who was worried to come to talk and see the facilities. A few did come. The petition is still by the bedside of the person who initiated it.

Perhaps the experience of Cooper Street and of the prayer counselling have given an added expectation of God's healing. A monthly healing service began in February 1993. Because Jesus Christ's commission to his disciples to go into all the world to preach and heal applies to every Christian, all the church members can take it in turn to be part of the ministering teams at the Communion rail.

Gordon Barley is enthusiastic. 'It's a way of bringing the love of Christ to non-Christians in the community, especially those that are going through depression, bereavement or emotional traumas. Just to have a hand placed on their shoulder and reassuring words, and receiving prayers. There's also the opportunity for them to be followed up as well. To receive counselling.'

• • •

It is important for evangelism. At each of the last four healing services a new person has become a Christian. There haven't been dramatic physical healings but there have been significant improvements. Edward Furness gave testimony that his hay fever had been cured. Pat Lynch remembers praying for him at the previous service. As she prayed for Edward she had a strong sense that she was being persecuted and left out of things. 'It was in my imagination really. I came to the realization that before I went up for prayer when Edward said what would you like to be prayed for, I was going to ask for this persecution thing. I knew the Lord saved me because I felt such a warmth go through me at the realization of it. But he did pray for me. I'm now talking to people that I wasn't talking to. I know many people have been helped through this prayer healing.'

In the end empowering is a matter of confidence. This is true whether the task is classed as spiritual or non-spiritual. Carol Forza, for example, was asked to be responsible for the letting of the six rooms at the top of Vincent Street which had been empty and redecorated. She said,

'I was quite taken aback because I thought how could I possibly? Me? I went "Wow", I'll have to go away and suss this out a little. So I went away and I prayed and God anointed me. I was anointed for the work so I knew definitely He wanted me to do that. It's helped me too, although I'm not on a wage, to go into a working environment, to work with people in a work situation which I'd never done before. Although I've taken on bits of responsibility since I've become a Christian, this is actually a big jump, in saying you're ready and I was quite shocked that people thought I was that ready.'

. . .

Betty Tyson remembers:

'I'd never worked in an office. As for answering the telephone – the only time I answered a phone was the one indoors. I found it strange at first that you could get paid for talking to someone on the phone. I enjoyed it as long as they gave me something to do. I got on very well with the old people. I chatted to them. I worked half a day on this community project for a year. Done some office work – done some filing. Then when I was asked to stay on for Mayflower and do Advice Desk updates and filing, I said I didn't really think I could do it. They said I'd been doing it all the time!'

. . .

Betty still finds it difficult to call herself a community worker because she thought community workers would have lots of training. But she acknowledges she has been on courses to do with welfare rights, pensioners, benefits, debt counselling, AIDS awareness, drugs and booze. She likes her job. What about branching out to something else? 'Funny enough, just recently Edward pointed out a job. It was £12,000 a year working with Community Links. So I said, "Could be I'd only spend it! I like it here." '

Grace Raggett remembers Alice Meakins serving in the launderette. She had never had contact with people in that way before.

'**Sometimes to people** she seemed very hard to understand but she had a heart of gold. Under the exterior of trying to be hard, if she saw anybody come in there, just a little thing like they couldn't afford a cup of tea, she'd say, "I don't think they've got any money, Grace." She'd just go over and say "Can I come and sit and have a cup of tea with you. Would you like one?" '

• • •

Barbara Graham has been teaching herself the guitar and loves music.

'**It helps me** tremendously, it's not just that you play the songs, look at the music and just play; you actually listen. My favourite songs are the ones I like the words to. You read the words as well as the music. I find it a very good way of worshipping.' She talks about the children's involvement. 'We have a time of worship in the children's group, learning them new songs and them singing, 'cos I think children find it very embarrassing to sing. I did. So it's getting used to singing and we teach them instruments as far as we can. We're not all brilliant musicians.'

• • •

A group working with the elderly has been run by local people for a long time. Mary Middleton, Gwen Levett and others in addition to the Lunch Club have organized a weekly meeting on Tuesday evenings and another on Wednesday afternoons for over twenty years. Many outings are arranged in the summer and for a number of years Mary organized a two-week holiday for pensioners, making the bookings, organizing the transport and collecting the money. In the last few years she has been giving a stronger spiritual input to Wednesday Mums as she has an increasing confidence to speak.

The growing confidence has meant people are willing not just to do readings or lead prayers, but also lead services and develop music and even drama. Mary Middleton regularly leads the evening service and on the last occasion there was widespread comment on an almost tangible sense of the Lord's presence during the worship. John Dove preached that evening on patience, part of the fruit of the Holy Spirit. There was spontaneous applause when he finished. The following Sunday morning after the congregation had broken into groups to discuss the theme of worship, five different people wanted to come forward to speak of how the Lord had touched their lives in the last week.

A number of people have commented on Doreen Turner's leading of evening worship. As well as the lively songs she practically always includes a sketch or a dramatized reading. But it is not all swinging from the chandeliers and there are precious times of open prayer, communion and quieter singing. The teaching and preaching of God's Word, however, remain central to the worship.

What of the youth work? Towards the end of 1991 the church felt sufficiently strong to reopen the doors of the club to local kids, starting with a small nucleus from church families. Juniors quickly grew to forty, inters to ninety. Attempts were made at senior work but sustaining leadership for it was difficult. There is no paid youth leader. There are just the two clubs each week staffed by local church members with smaller groups being taken away to Asheldham, the Chelmsford diocesan centre in Essex. This has been sustained for over two years now. It still isn't easy.

In the summer of 1993 a visit from seventeen of the Street Invaders from British Youth for Christ resulted in a group of local youngsters responding to the gospel. They are now meeting weekly together. On a recent visit to Asheldham, John Dove was sitting on the top bunk sharing his story of Jesus with five very attentive teenagers. The work is small. It is too early to assess its effectiveness. It is taking its place alongside the other activities of the Centre as part of the outreach of a locally run church in the area.

Despite all the work, the church and Centre remain very fragile. With the departure of those who could now be in leadership, it has not been easy to train up new leaders. Fears and lack of confidence remain. New people have come through the commitment course each year to join the committed membership, but some have not renewed after a year or two. There is a danger that aiming at high standards can reinforce failure.

Is there the danger that Mayflower gets bogged down with the problems of those needing care at the expense of the 'happy pagans' of the original vision. In some ways, yes, but it seems to have been God's direction and a natural outcome of its setting in Canning Town to be a place of healing and sanctuary. Does that mean losing the cutting edge of evangelism into the community? Perhaps it did for a while as Mayflower went through all the changes. It is placed in an increasingly broken community, one which is in desperate need of anchors, stability and hope. As an increasing number of people find that hope in Jesus, it will be a place for them. This year's commitment course consists of six — Sean who was in prison for child abuse, James who came to us from hospital after attempted suicide, Dave who spent many years living under cardboard on the streets as an alcoholic, Jean who has been married and divorced three times, Peter who has been fostered out since he was two to many different families and institutions and Erica who is black and has had the most stable of all the backgrounds. Each one has been touched by God recently and come into a real experience of being 'born again' and the meetings are very rich.

St Paul writes that he prayed to the Lord three times to take away his 'thorn in the flesh'. But God's answer was 'My grace is all you need, for my power is greatest when you are weak.'[2] Mayflower Christians can join with Paul in being proud of their weaknesses and brokenness in order to feel the protection of Christ's power over them. 'For when we are weak, then we are strong.'

The Love that Lasts a Lifetime
Doreen Turner

I was fifteen when I first went to Mayflower Youth Club – that was some thirty-two years ago. George Burton was the youth leader. I began by going to the open youth club and after a couple of visits to the club was asked if I would like to join the Sunday Group who used to meet in Mr Burton's flat. I then got to know Jean Lodge Patch (as she was then). Jean was the assistant youth worker. I very quickly began to realize that she was a very special person, one of those people you meet and there is something different about them. That difference was the fact that she had Jesus in her life. Jesus just oozed from her. I became quite excited about Jesus and what he could do in my life. Perhaps I could have the same sparkle that Jean had? I gave my life to Jesus on my knees in Jean's bedroom about three months after I first came to Mayflower.

It wasn't long before I got involved in the youth work. I began by running a group for girls of eleven or over; the purpose of the group was to introduce the youngsters to Jesus. I belonged to the Sunday Group and was being nurtured in my Christian life in that group and at the same time ran a group that I was seeing converted and I helped them. Many teenagers came to the Lord through those groups. We did many things together, went on holidays abroad, went camping – you know those camps where a gnat always manages to find its way into your sleeping bag – you never do find out if it's after your blood or it's just damn cold. Either way you end up with masses of bites in the most awkward places. All the activities had some kind of Christian input and there were strict rules about drink (not so much drugs in those days) and definitely no canoodling with the opposite sex. The favourite saying of Mr Burton's was 'familiarity breeds contempt' and so a tight rein was kept on courting couples.

I still believe, looking back, that the groups were more successful than the open clubs because of the time given to individuals and Mr Burton's success was because of the fact that he was like a dad to many of us; he definitely loved us and we knew it.

I met my husband, Bill, in the Sunday Group. We started courting when I was seventeen, got engaged at eighteen and we married when I was twenty. Bill was twenty-three. He too had been converted at Mayflower and helped with the youth work. In fact, he enjoyed youth work so much that he decided he would like to be a youth and community worker himself. He was encouraged to go to college for training which at the time was quite difficult because by then we had two small children; but we got by. I'm not sure if the Lord meant Bill to do youth work. I think at the time we felt it to be right, but looking at the devastation it caused in our lives I have often wondered if we had got it wrong or whether Satan was determined to destroy what God wanted to do to fulfil Mayflower's vision of local leadership. Bill got his diploma and was now a qualified youth and community worker. Mayflower had a vacancy for a youth worker so everything seemed to fit into place. This is when our problems began. We gave our council house up and moved into Mayflower. Not long after moving in, Rosy Finch, the other youth worker left, which left Bill to run the clubs with the residents from the Vincent Street hostel along with some of the local church members.

At the time Bill was the only male member of staff who lived in Mayflower, apart from the warden, Denis Downham, who was soon to leave. During this time the Holy Spirit had begun to move in a new way in the church. A small number of the congregation had begun to exercise the gifts of the Spirit. (Many residents who had been to Mayflower had been baptized in the Spirit but were told at their interview that they were not to speak to the local people about the Holy Spirit.) But the Lord introduced us to his Holy Spirit in His own way and in His own time regardless of the residents' brief. At this time I was having a prayer meeting each Sunday evening after church in my house and we were experiencing the Lord speaking to us in a new way. I remember the first picture I had of Viv Abrahams kneeling before the Cross and sure enough not long after that Viv came to the Lord.

Well, we know where God moves, so does Satan, to destroy what the Lord wants to do and that was exactly what was happening. Lots of the Christian female residents seemed to have problems and wanted Bill's shoulder to cry on. Satan knew what he was doing. Bill, I think, felt quite flattered by the attention of these young ladies and missing his youth because his father had walked out and left him as the eldest of eight to take much of the responsibility for the family, he now began to realize he was popular and liked by the residents and was tempted by the young girls showing they liked him. Satan found a weakness and cashed in on it. This was our family's downfall. Bill ended up sleeping with two or three of these young, middle-class, Christian girls who came to do their bit for Canning Town. Our marriage ended, we lost our home and Bill lost his job. Our family became an embarrassment to Mayflower. Some tried to encourage us to move out of Canning Town. Canning Town was our home, all my family and friends lived in Canning Town. I didn't want to move to another area where I knew no one and although I tried to patch things up with Bill, I believe I was too immature to deal with the problem in the right way and couldn't accept what had happened.

We rowed almost each day – no way to bring children up – and so we parted. Where was all this forgiveness and never-ending love that we had heard about for so many years; had the Lord deserted us? No, He hadn't, but the Christians had. So I went away from the Lord for about eight years. Those eight years were the worst eight years of my life. In 1986, I came back to Mayflower and to the Lord. I can only speak for myself, but it's as if my faith has come alive. I can hear the Lord's voice, I can feel His presence. I feel His overwhelming love and I feel overwhelmed at times by the love I feel for Him. God has gifted me to serve Him and that is my heart's desire.

We as a church are beginning to look at ourselves, to let God deal with me (us) and to stand together in the power of the Holy Spirit, beginning to really love each other, wanting to support each other. I believe the gifts of the spirit are really important to the church. I know we need to be careful because again church members can become jealous of each other but I have seen people come to Jesus because of a word of knowledge, people healed and set free because of the gifts of the Spirit being used to glorify God.

In years gone by many promises have been made by God for Mayflower and even before Mayflower for Canning Town. We can't expect to walk our own way and still receive the fulfilment of those promises. Are we prepared to walk his narrow way or are the things of the world too glamorous?

Mayflower used to have a high profile in David Sheppard's day, the place was teeming with people, the buildings buzzing with life. A large team of dedicated full-time workers gave their all to the work; but what about behind the scenes? Being a local staff member was quite an eye-opener. That united front portrayed to the local people wasn't as united as it was made out to be, and over the years more and more things have come to light.

One of the biggest shocks to me (apart from what my own family encountered) was Jean and David Hewitt's book about Mr Burton. It recorded what went on in the background with the staff. We teenagers were completely unaware of those events. We all knew Mr Burton had a temper and if you upset him, you knew it, but for us it was soon over. But some of the staff obviously went through hell and that continued for others in different ways.

It's been a battle that's been going on for years between God and Satan, and most of us over the years, instead of fighting in that battle, have been unaware that it has been going on – until the last few years where God's Spirit has been directing us to pray against spiritual forces that have held us and trapped us for years. Lives have been ruined by debt, immorality, greed. People have been oppressed and have responded by rebelling or becoming apathetic and giving up, committing suicide, taking drugs, drinking, trying to escape the reality of the hopelessness of the situations they find themselves in, marriages breaking down, people afraid to marry, living together hoping it will work out, children having two mums or two dads or a single parent many of whom find they can't cope.

For God to fulfil the vision of the Mayflower for local people to take leadership positions and the responsibilities that go with those positions, we have got to break through the barriers, rise above these situations and support each other. There are many talented people in Canning Town. Jesus is our Rock, Jesus is our Strength, our confidence is in Him. He is our hope and our Salvation. Every time a local person starts moving forward and is given responsibility it's as if Satan targets us and all our weaknesses are played on, and this is the time we need to come together with others and pray to look to the Lord to give us a way out, a way through and to stand instead of falling and going to pieces like we have in the past. We wanted this book to be honest, to portray a true picture of what's happened over the years. Well the truth is not pretty, it's not easy being a Christian and we have all suffered from battle fatigue from the wounds received battling in this place, both people in the past and the present. We can go on being the walking wounded or we can let go of the past and walk free, healed, restored, transformed, forgiven. Almost every youth leader that has worked at Mayflower has left devastated and broken in some way.

Other members of staff, even past wardens, have suffered because of their time here, unable to cope, unable to resist temptation. This goes for residents that have lived in the hostel. They have gone away full of guilt, shamed: remember it is Satan that has caused these things to happen. He is the tempter; our flesh is weak; either way, we are fighting not flesh and blood but principalities and spiritual forces. Ephesians 6:11-13.

As I laid down the bad feelings, the resentment, anger, hurt of the happenings of the past, repented and drew closer to the Lord, He began to open doors to minister to people by the gifts of the Spirit. It was exciting learning to listen when praying instead of reeling off a shopping list and feeling elated that I could hear the Lord's voice. He began to use me in prophecy, words of knowledge. As soon as I turned to Him and started praying, sheepishly I tried to speak in tongues, the tongue that he had gifted me with all those years before, and sure enough the gift was still available to be used. What a merciful Lord we have.

This is how good God is. I had been back at Mayflower about five years when I was asked to be a leader and the Lord had begun to challenge me about giving up my job. I had a good job as assistant coordinator on a large YTS scheme and was buying my house, but the Lord had other plans - plans for me to work in the Sanctuary. So I began a pilot project over the New Hunt 'Freedom House' and right from day one I was experiencing new things. He was teaching me. I'd not come across drug withdrawal, possessison, child abuse, the occult and here it was, all together under the one roof.

Those first few months were extremely difficult for me. I have always hated confrontation of any kind, but this was a situation where you had to confront. I was beginning to recognize when someone was out of their head on drugs, how deceitful they could be, and then I can remember praying for someone who was possessed, an icy cold air going from my feet upwards, an evil spirit trying to stop me praying, using fear. Oh, yes, I was scared to death to begin with. I then realized that the Lord was in control. He loved me and wasn't going to let anything happen to me. Since then I have seen numerous manifestations - horrible, sickening sights, things I do not like and could well do without. But my confidence is in the Lord.

As long as I'm looking to Him and being guided by His Holy Spirit I have nothing to fear. I consider it a privilege to pray for people and it's a lovely experience to see someone set free from demon possession, hurt, guilt and to see their faces when they witness the Lord moving in power.

I believe the Lord has already used my bad experiences to enable me to help others in a similar boat. Sometimes we don't see what the Lord is doing, but quite often we can look back and see what He has done. I pray we will continue to see our Lord at work in Power at Mayflower, transforming lives, enabling us to stand in the name of Jesus, walking on, not going round in circles. If we are able to be honest enough to share the things that trouble us, the things that tempt us, those skeletons in the cupboard that cause us to feel guilty, I believe the circle can be broken because Satan will no longer have a foothold to bring us down.

We need words of blessing not cursing to enable us to move on without seeing more lives broken. Let God have His way and life at Mayflower will radiate with the light of the Lord and shine out in the darkness to allow the people in Canning Town to see the Lord at work, leaving behind the devastation and hopelessness coming into a NEW LIFE.

I'm here for a laugh

Can Dreams Come True?

THE VISION ADOPTED in 1985 ends with the words '. . . our major concern is not with methods and strategies but with being a visible alternative to the sickness of society around us, to be a sign and evidence of what God is doing and will do.' Running through the story of the last hundred years has been clear evidence of that sickness. The oppression that has led to apathy and rebellion, the broken spirit which has given up in large measure and relapsed into self-centred dependency, the self-preserving hardness which blots out love and tenderness, the particular effect on male and female which has led to the distortion of relationships and the devastating break-up of marriages and families, the drift into drugs, petty crime and violence.

We have the most precious and wonderful answer to that sickness in the person of Jesus Christ, the one who said he had come to set at liberty the oppressed, to heal the broken-hearted and to open the eyes of the blind. Those of us who have experienced new birth in him know that those are not just words but the deepest truth. As we have surrendered our lives to him we have received back infinitely more — release from greed and selfishness, the taking away of hopelessness and futility, the softening of our hard hearts and a new love and sense of fulfilment. That is what we have to share. It is in the end the only final solution worth pursuing.

But it isn't a private matter. When the Holy Spirit came at Pentecost it was a very public affair and the way the Christians organized their lives could be seen by all. It is no good our protesting about injustice in society, greed and selfishness if there is no visible alternative in the church to demonstrate a different way. Mayflower has sought to be evidence of that different way over its history — trying to reach those who would otherwise never go near a church, getting involved in messy, painful situations to demonstrate that there is a love that can overcome evil, hatred, rejection and worthlessness and loss.

We have had different emphases at different stages of our life. In recent years we have changed our structures, firstly to become a functioning community together more than an institutional organization and secondly to counteract the inherited oppression and dependency by putting the main decision-making into the hands of the local Christians. We have counteracted the exploitation of the area by introducing an equal-pay policy. We have counteracted the hardness and hopelessness around us by opening up as a place of healing a sanctuary offering hope and love. We have witnessed in our dealings with one another that there are right and wrong actions, behaviour, relationships. In our own brokenness we can affirm the power of forgiveness and healing. All of that has come not from our own efforts, cleverness or courage but from the work of God through the Holy Spirit moving in our lives. Particularly in the last two years we have had to face again our own weaknesses and vulnerability as God has refined us, sometimes very painfully.

Where do we go from here? Perhaps the greatest breakdown here has been in family life, once the East End's strongest asset. We are a Family Centre and at the heart is Jesus and his family. The danger in families is either that they become so exclusive that no one outside the family is given attention or that though the family lives under the same roof it is only as a matter of convenience because everyone does their own thing. The family of God has a strong bond holding it together. Paul writes of the Unity which the Spirit of God brings. We have one Lord, one faith, one hope, one baptism. We have a shared set of values. We are bound together in love and peace. Within that there are individual differences, different talents and gifts, different roles, men and women taking their places alongside each other, the young and the old, black, white and brown, the educated and the illiterate, all with their own part to play but within the one family in rightful relationship and submission to one another.

That isn't easy to achieve and this side of heaven there will always be bits out of joint or not functioning properly. But at Mayflower we have a unique set of buildings and people set in a particularly needy inner-city area of Canning Town. We are open seven days a week and have the opportunity to demonstrate a family life to bring hope and challenge to our neighbourhood that many other churches do not. We aren't a community all living on a single site and self-contained, taken out of the world where if people come they do so on our terms for the time we decide. Nor are we the church on the corner where people just go on Sundays and perhaps one mid-week meeting.

How far should the family commitment to each other go? The family is not there for itself. Jesus gave us the commission to go into all the world and preach the gospel, make disciples, heal and deliver. Paul writes of the privileges of taking to non-Christians the good news about the infinite riches of Christ. That can happen in and through all the activities and facilities of the Centre open freely to all; it can happen as we share open-air worship in Rathbone Market and as we show care and concern for people in their own homes and families. In the early Mayflower days there

Mayflower in bloom – 1992

was a heavy emphasis on reaching families and seeing Christian homes opened up for hospitality to neighbours. But history, as well as Scripture shows that this is most effective where the bond between the Christians is strongest. The visible unity and love between the Christians has a powerful effect. Jesus said that by our unity and love for one another people would believe in him. That bond needs constant nourishment through worship, prayer, teaching and fellowship and these are all emphasized in our commitment to each other. How far should that be complemented by a closer social life, sharing of possessions and money? Only God can show us that in His time. If you work consciously at creating a community, that can often replace God at the centre. It is out of our love for Him and one another that the right structures emerge.

There is, however, a real danger that the community turns in on itself and becomes ingrown. Paradoxically it is local people born and brought up in the area who often have the greatest fear of violence or taking risks. This is why when violence has erupted in club or elsewhere it has often been left to external staff and residents to cope with. Local response to difficulties is firstly, 'it shouldn't be allowed', followed by banning and closing. There is a constant need for us to help each other overcome our fears. It has been said, 'Faith is spelt R—I—S—K.' There is always a bias towards the safe and comfortable. With the things that have happened in the last few years we haven't been allowed to be too comfortable but the Centre needs to be constantly opened up with fresh air blowing through it to make us sensitive to the needs of all. There has been the danger of taking on too much and overstretching people and that still remains the case. But we also need to beware of fossilizing.

In 1988 I wrote, 'I have a dream that one day instead of money being given to the East End, the East End will be sending money to those in even greater physical need. Instead of receiving workers and missionaries, the East End will be sending out not the odd individual who has broken the mould but teams of people to other parts of the country in greater spiritual need.'

We have seen the beginning of that. Following the trip to Rumania in November we are grappling with the possibility of joint projects with the churches there, raising more money here, sending more local people with skills who could help.

We do not see these things happening on our own. In our relationships with the other Custom House and Canning Town churches and wider through Newham Christian Fellowship we are joining hands with others across the different denominations in prayer, worship, evangelism, celebration, training, aid and open-air marches and witness. Part of the work of God prophesied in Ezekial 36 is the bringing together of his scattered people and this new-found unity is a realization of that.

One of the problems is that we need more Christians. Betty Tyson said, 'If more people became Christians so there are more people involved and you could start doing more things on a Christian basis.' How will this happen? We have seen a few people become Christians each year recently. But looking back over the history of the place and the hardness of the area, we know that our own strategies and techniques will not provide the answer. Hannah Watherston says: 'It depends utterly on a supernatural move of God to quicken the church into amazing work — work that we can't achieve on our own anyway — I see the future. It can only go forward. I would like to see us daring to do much more in terms of our faith in God that's been building particularly over the last four or five years. People's awareness of God is much more, for them it's growing. When we have a problem, either financial or physical, God isn't the last person we turn to. I'd like to see that element of faith that's actually quite small burst out on the church and see God honouring that faith.'

Again history has shown that revival has not broken out in the expected places, where churches are full, where there is a lot of activity. One of the songs we sing is, 'Where darkness has been darkest, the brightest light will shine.' Ezekiel in Chapter 36 quoted in the first chapter of this book, having described the devastation and destruction, says he is going to act not for the sake of the Isrealites who have turned away from him and disgraced him but for the sake of his holy name, so that everyone would know that he was the Lord. It will not be because we are any more deserving than any other part of this country. We have turned our backs on God as much as anywhere. But where the oppression has been greatest, where the people have had the least ability to stand on their own feet, that is often where God chooses to send his revival power because there is no way human beings will take the credit for it.

We do not sit here thinking there is nothing we can do until revival comes. We need to get on with the things we believe God is asking us to do. But in the Ezekiel passage when God moves He brings together His people who have been scattered. He will sprinkle clean water to make them clean, He will take out the stubborn heart of stone and give them a new soft obedient heart of flesh and He will put His spirit within them to do all that He asks of them. Ezekiel adds that in addition the yield of the fields and corn and the fruit trees will increase, the ruins will be rebuilt and the cities which were torn down, looted and left in ruins will be inhabited and fortified.

Chris Timothy says: 'What I'd really love to see and I hope and pray I will, is the church packed. Not just with people coming out of curiosity but people coming 'coz they want to worship the Lord. And I think that'll be the day when I will really burst into tears of joy.'

We believe that won't just be a lot of people in a church building. It will have an impact on this area, where God has called us to build His kingdom, changing much that is hard, self-centred and greedy into what is soft, loving and generous. Is that simply a pipe dream and a fantasy to keep our spirits up? What we do know is that it is only the work God does which has any lasting value. So we read in the last book of the Bible. 'Yes, indeed I am coming soon!' and our response is, 'So be it. Come, Lord Jesus!'

Appendix

VISION STATEMENT ADOPTED IN SEPTEMBER
1985

The need

Our task is to proclaim and live out the Kingdom of God. That Kingdom, Jesus said, is one in which prisoners are released, the blind see, the deaf hear, the oppressed are set at liberty, the broken-hearted are healed and the poor have good news preached to them. We live in a society which is in desperate need of that Kingdom. Many people's lives here and elsewhere are crippled by broken family relationships and marriages, by drink and drugs, by materialism and greed, by the occult, by disease, loneliness, fear and despair. Communities are crippled by hatred and hostility, often racial in character, leading to violence and crime, by hopelessness generated by unemployment and bad housing. Behind these factors — whether structural, family or personal — we recognize that Satan is holding people in suspicion and fear.

The response

We believe that amongst all the needs of our community the fundamental one is reconciliation with God. This involves repentance, faith, baptism, and the filling of His Holy Spirit. God is capable of breaking in at all levels in our own and our community life — physically, emotionally, mentally, spiritually, structurally — to bring change and healing. This can take place both by natural and by supernatural means.

We are to love one another

We, as Christians, are called to be part of His Church in our area. That involves us in personal and corporate discipleship — in worship and prayer, in sharing unreservedly with each other all we have and possess, in forgiveness and accepting one another, in being ready to lay down even our lives for one another. We need to love one another as Jesus Christ loves us, and we can only do that through His Spirit.

We are to build our life together

Our life together as God's family is very important. We seek to recognize the different natural and spiritual gifts: we give opportunity to exercise them. We encourage ministries to build up and unite us. We are organized, and yet changing and dynamic as we discern God's will for us.

We are to live God's way

We live by God's standards which are very different from those of the world around us and yet we are open to our local community. We put up no barriers, and have no bias to one class or culture, and witness that in God's Kingdom there are no distinctions on the basis of class, colour, sex or age.

We are to love our neighbour

We are to love our neighbour as ourselves, which means seeking for him or her what we would have ourselves. The different aspects of our work seek to provide opportunities for physical, educational and emotional development. We provide facilities, we seek to build up confidence and ability. We want to stand with those who are weak — in their desire for justice, for dignity and for security. That will involve us in the sacrifice of time, energy, resources and sometimes our reputation and our own security.

We are to share our faith

Our desire is that men and women should come to experience the reality of the Kingdom of God in their own lives. However, our evangelism is not primarily a programme, but a natural expression of the hope that lives within us. Our major concern is not with methods and strategies but with being a visible alternative to the sickness of society around us, being a sign and evidence of what God is doing and will do.

August 1985

Notes

Chapter 1

1. *Household Words* – a weekly journal conducted by Charles Dickens, 12th September 1887.
2. Reginald Kennedy Cox, *An Autobiography,* (Hodder and Stoughton, 1934) p. 13.
3. R. Douglas Brown, *The Port of London* (Terence Dalton Limited, 1978) p. 148.
4. *Mayflower News,* May 1984.

Chapter 2

1. Ben T. Tinton, *War Comes to the Docks* (Marshall, Morgan and Scott, 1941) pp.21-2.
2. Reproduced in *Old Malvernian* (1893).
3. *Old Malvernian* (1898).
4. Reginald Kennedy Cox, *Docklands Saga* (1955), p. 30.
5. Reginald Kennedy Cox, *An Autobiography* (Hodder and Stoughton 1934) p. 251.
6. *Mayflower Log,* Winter 1961.
7. Reginald Kennedy Cox, *Docklands Saga* (1955) p. 66.
8. Ibid., p. 67.
9. Ibid., p. 49.
10. Ibid., p. 47.
11. Dockland Settlements Annual Report 1954.
12. *Mayflower News,* December 1987.

Chapter 3

1. Roland Allen, *Missionary Methods – St Paul's or Ours?* (World Dominion Press 1912) p. 81.
2. Ibid., p. 83.
3. George Burton, *People Matter More Than Things* (Hodder and Stoughton, 1965) p. 31.
4. Internal memo to Mayflower Council, local Committee and Staff, September 1962.
5. George Burton, *People Matter More Than Things* (Hodder and Stoughton, 1965), p. 107.
6. David Driscoll and Greg Smith, *West Ham Church Life Survey,* 1984, p. 33.

Chapter 4

1. George Burton, *People Matter More Than Things* (Hodder and Stoughton, 1965), p. 38.
2. Ibid., p. 54.
3. Ibid., p. 56–58.
4. Ibid., p. 58–59.
5. Ibid., p. 69.
6. Ibid., p. 73.
7. Ibid., p. 78.
8. Ibid., p. 104.
9. Ibid., p. 101.

Chapter 5

1. Compass: A report by the Redevelopment Working Party, December 1976, pp. 2, 5–6.
2. Ibid., p. 10.
3. *Mayflower News,* Winter 1977.
4. *Mayflower News,* April 1981.

Chapter 6

1. Youth Work Report 48, February 1985.
2. Youth Work Report 43, February 1984.
3. Youth Work Report 47, February 1984.
4. *Mayflower News,* May 1984.

5. Youth Work Report 44, June 1984.
6. Dimbleby Lecture, 1984.
7. Youth Work Report 37, September 1982.

Chapter 7

1. Rolland Allen, *Missionary Methods – St Paul's or Ours?* (World Dominion Press, 1912) p. 83.
2. Youth Work Report 47, October 1984.
3. *Mayflower News,* June 1989.
4. *Mayflower News,* December 1987.

Chapter 8

1. *Mayflower News,* December 1988.
2. 2 Corinthians 12:9.

Bibliography

George Burton, *People Matter More Than Things,* Hodder and
    Stoughton, 1965.
David and Jean Hewitt, *George Burton: A Study in Contradictions,*
    Hodder and Stoughton, 1969.
Reginald Kennedy Cox, *An Autobiography,* Hodder and
    Stoughton, 1934.
— *Docklands Saga,* 1955.
Roger Sainsbury, *Towards 1984,* Mayflower Family Centre, 1975.
David Sheppard, *Parson's Pitch,* Hodder and Stoughton, 1964.
— *Built as a City,* Hodder and Stoughton, 1975.
Ben T. Tinton, *War Comes to the Docks,* Marshall, Morgan and
    Scott, 1941.
Pip Wilson, *Gutter Feelings,* Hodder and Stoughton, 1985.